Arabic letters

My name is :   اسمي هو :

✿ Trace, Color & learn!

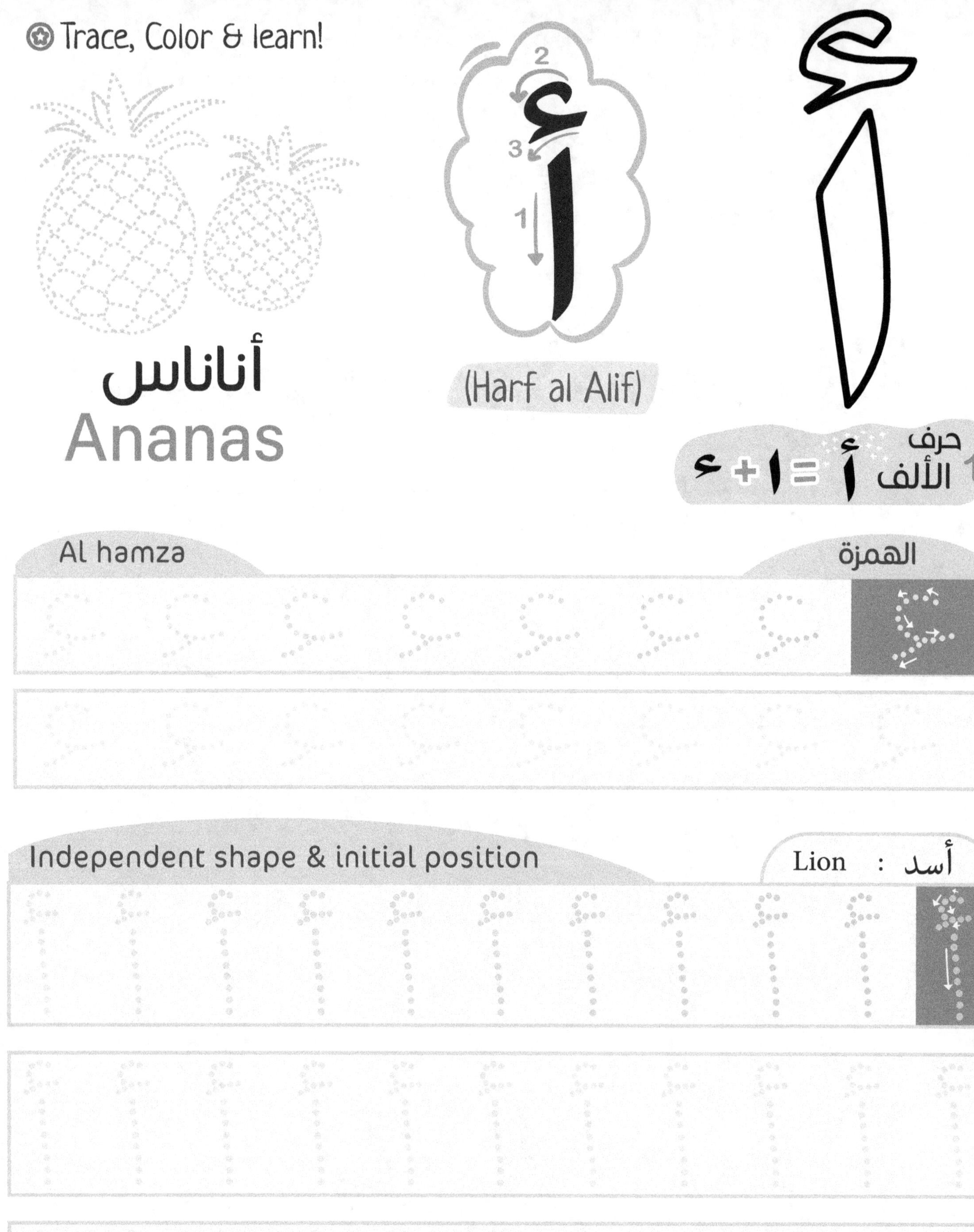

أناناس
Ananas
(Harf al Alif)
حرف الألف
1
أ + ١ = ء
Al hamza
الهمزة
Independent shape & initial position
Lion : أسد

Head : رأس

Medial position : ✗

Rust : صدأ

Final position : ✗

After connecting letters :

★ Alif is only connectable to the letter before (the letter to the right) ★

Mouse : فأر

Medial position :

News : نبأ

Final position :

◎ Let's practice !

⊛ Color the cirlces with letter Alif :

Couch
أريكة

⊛ Write the missing Alif letter :　　اكتب حرف الألف الناقص:

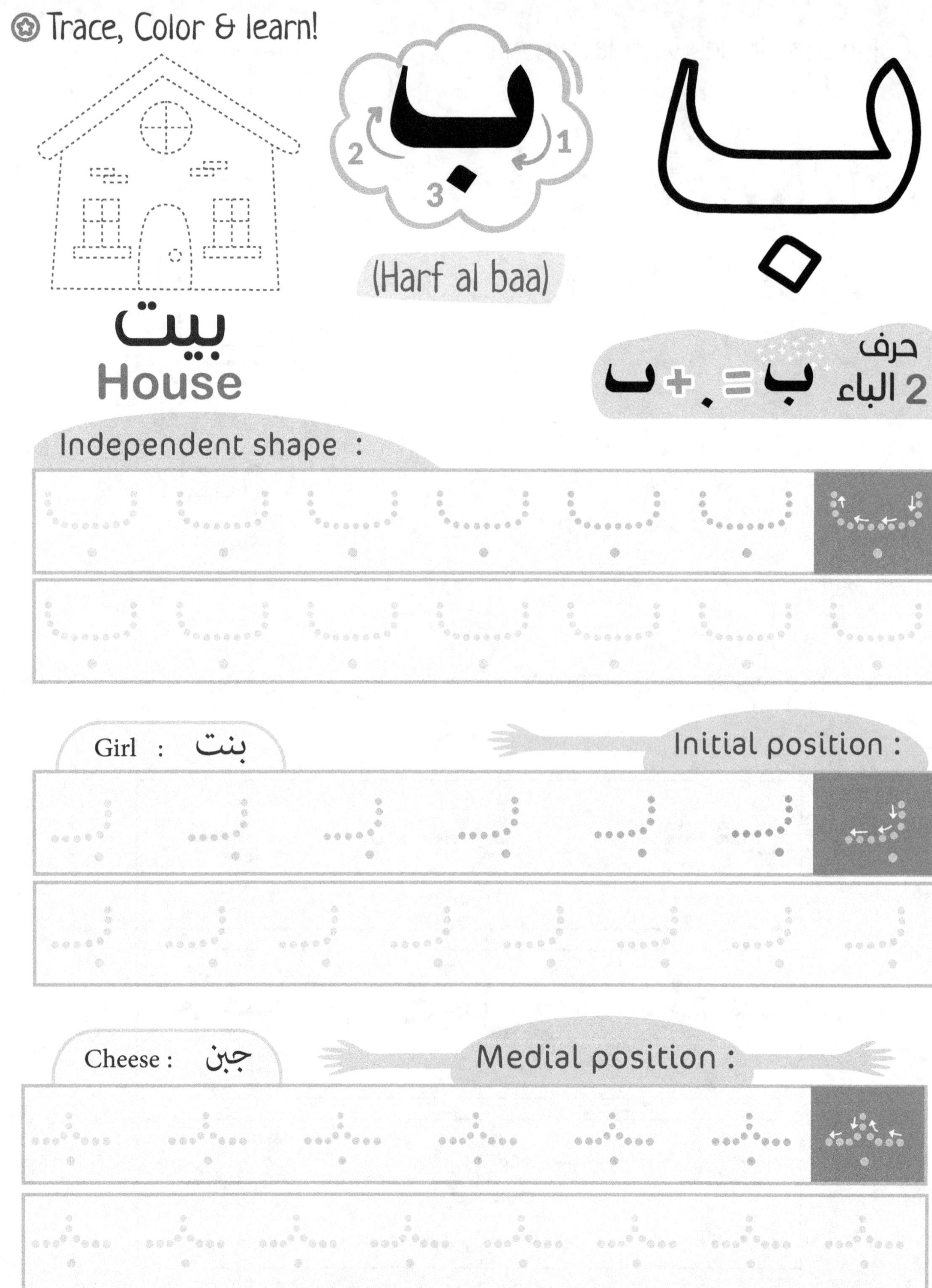
Trace, Color & learn!
House
بيت
ب
(Harf al baa)
2
3
1
ب ا
ب
حرف الباء 2
ب = . + ب
Independent shape :
Girl : بنت
Initial position :
Cheese : جبن
Medial position :

Dog : كلب

After nonconnecting letters : و،ذ،د،ر،ز،أ

Client : زبون

Book : كتاب

⊛ Let's practice !

Color the cirlces with letter Baa :

Write the missing Baa letter :

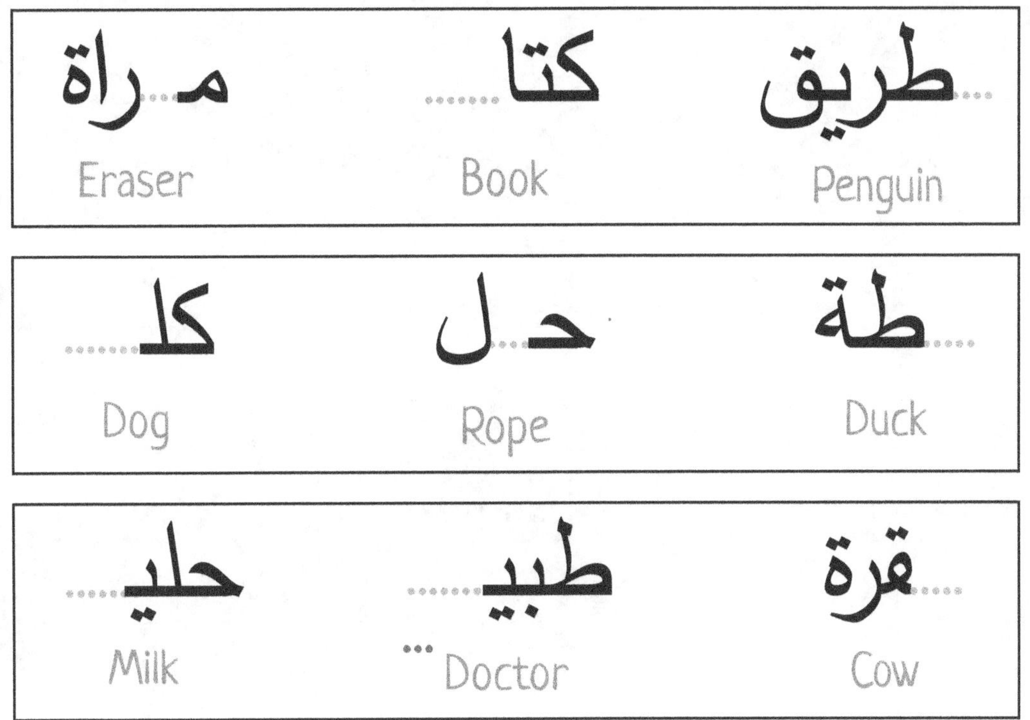

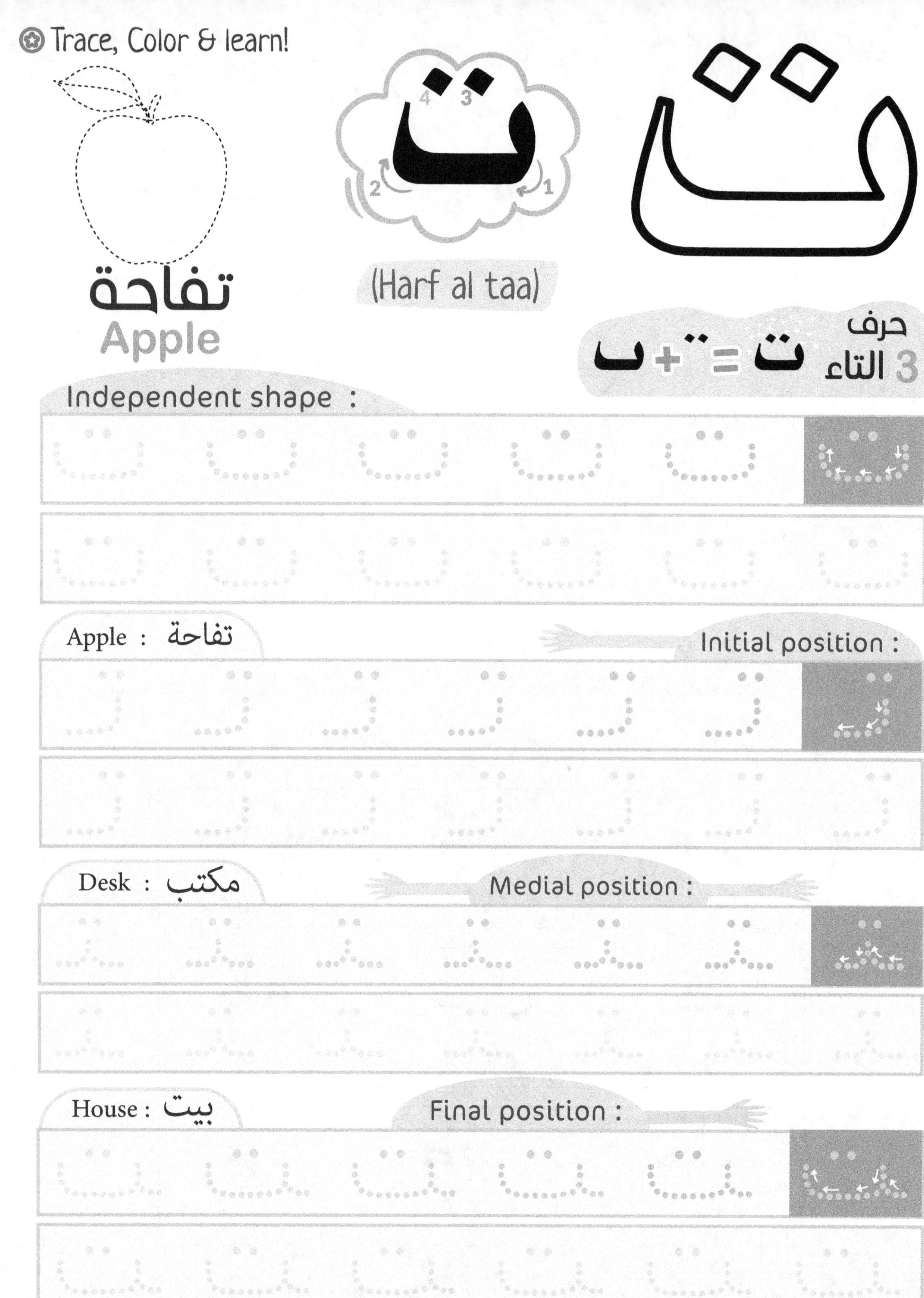

Trace, Color & learn!
تفاحة
Apple
(Harf al taa)
حرف التاء 3
ت = ˙˙ + ب
Independent shape :
Apple : تفاحة
Initial position :
Desk : مكتب
Medial position :
House : بيت
Final position :

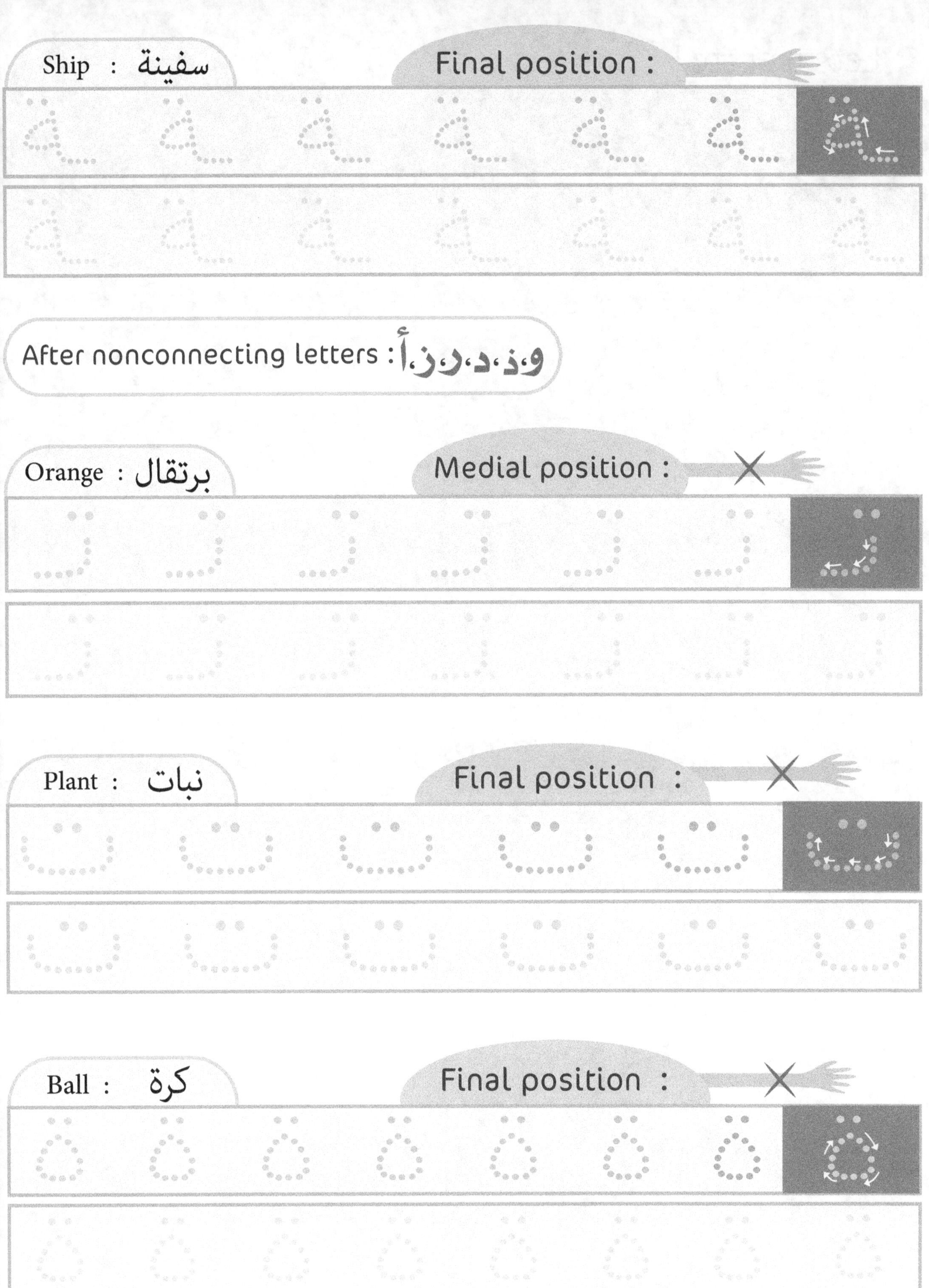

Ship : سفينة

Final position :

After nonconnecting letters : و، ذ، د، ر، ز، أ

Orange : برتقال

Medial position :

Plant : نبات

Final position :

Ball : كرة

Final position :

⊛ Let's practice !

● Color the ciricles with letter Taa :

● Write the missing Taa letter :

● اكتب حرف التاء الناقص:

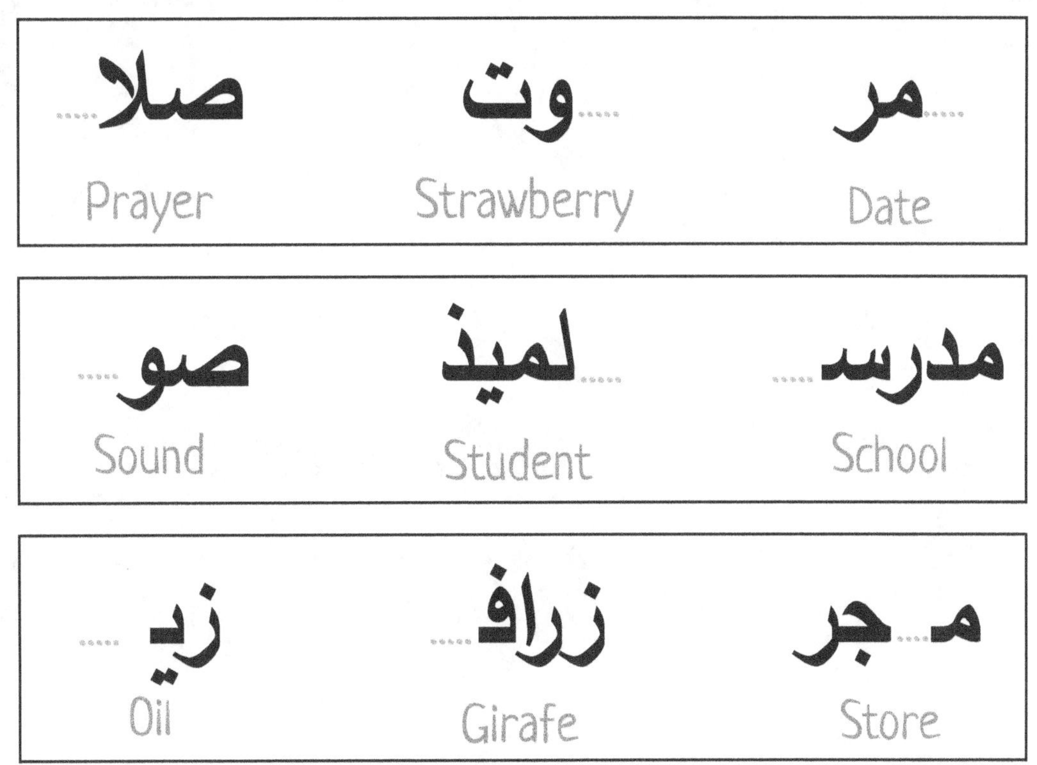

Trace, Color & learn!
3
ثلاثة
Three
ث ت
(Harf al thaa)
حرف الثاء 4 ث = ث + ب
Independent shape :
Precious : ثمين
Initial position :
Ice cream : مثلجات
Medial position :

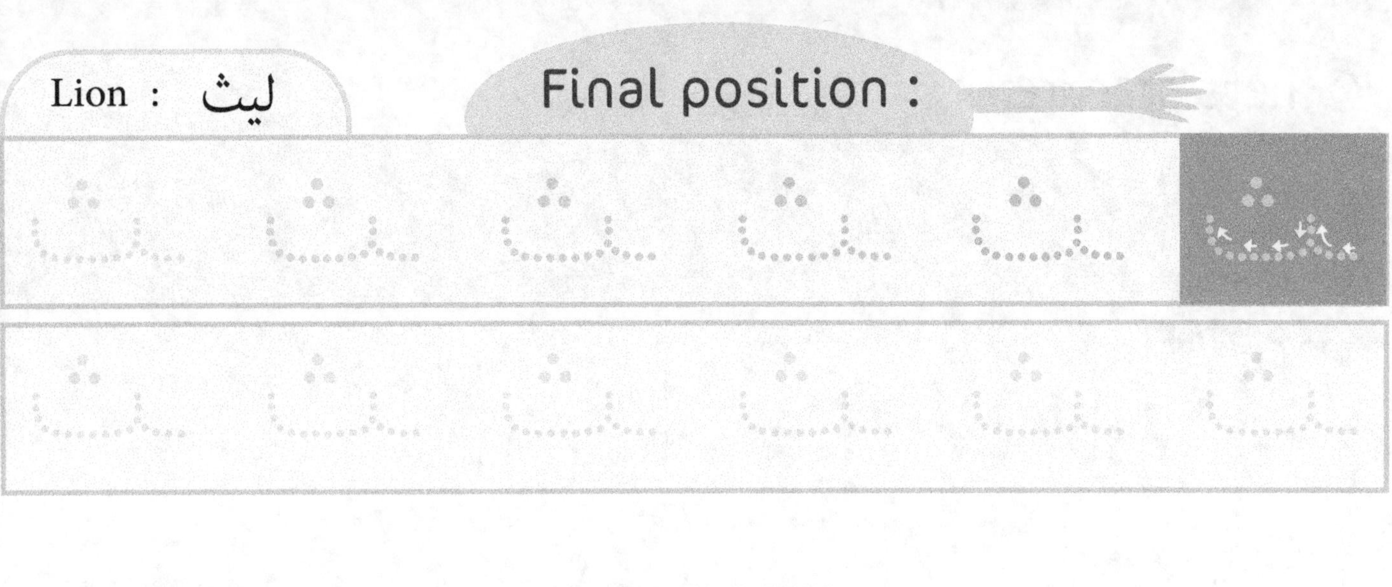

After nonconnecting letters : أ،ز،ر،د،ذ،و

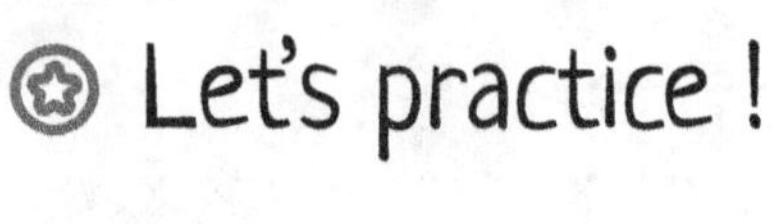
Let's practice !

◎ Color the ciricles with letter Thaa :

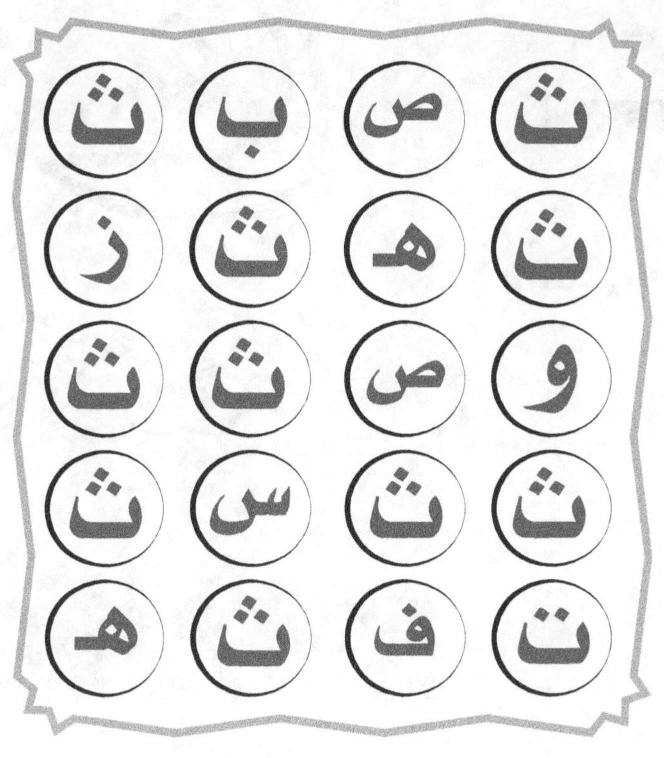

◎ Write the missing Thaa letter :   اكتب حرف الثاء الناقص: ◎

Trace, Color & learn!

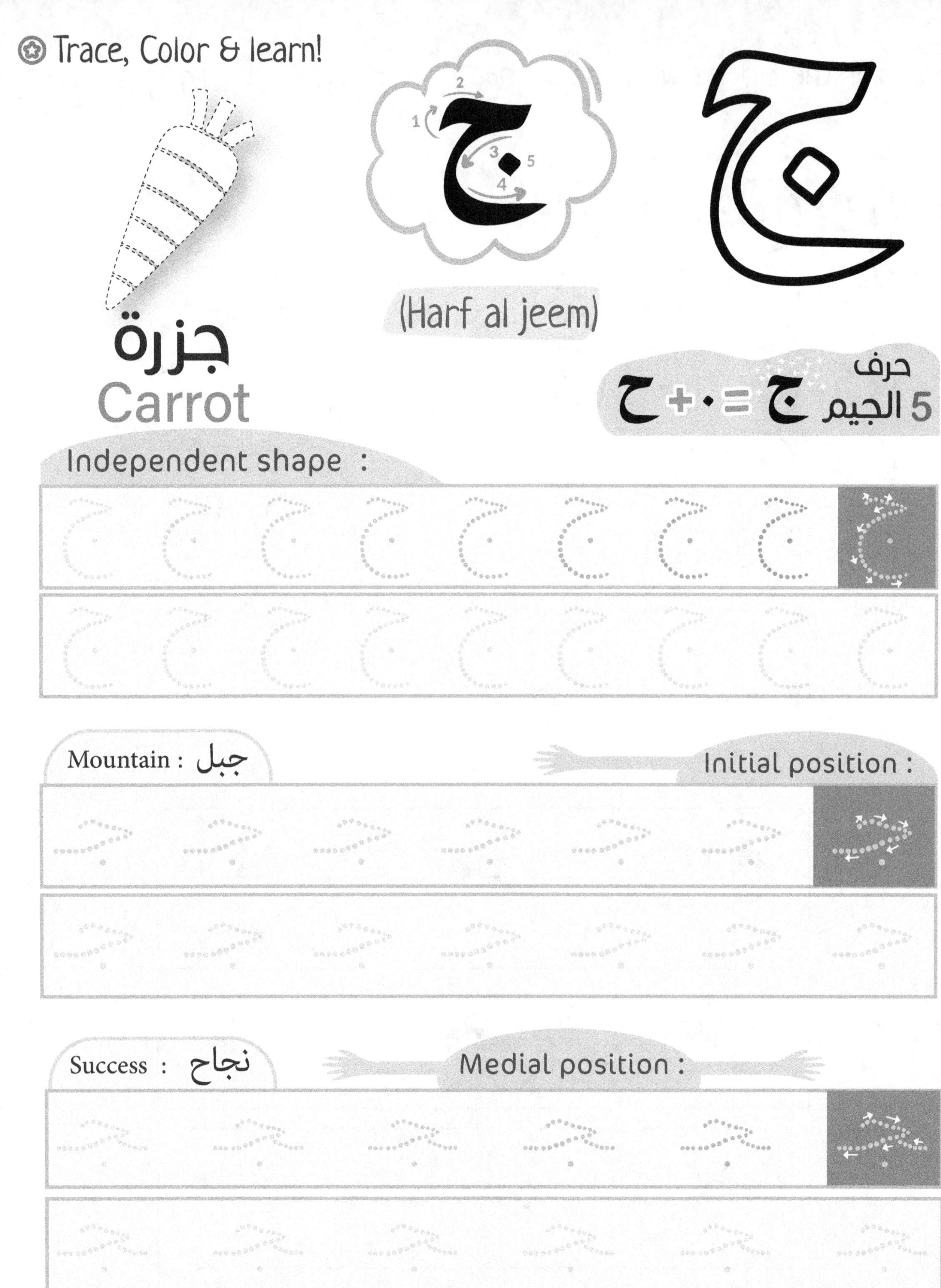
2
1
3 5
4
(Harf al jeem)
جزرة
Carrot
حرف الجيم 5 ج = ٠+ ح
Independent shape :
Mountain : جبل
Initial position :
Success : نجاح
Medial position :

Snow : ثلج

Final position :

After nonconnecting letters : و،ذ،د،ر،ز،أ

Face : وجه

Medial position :

Final position :

Tiarra : تاج

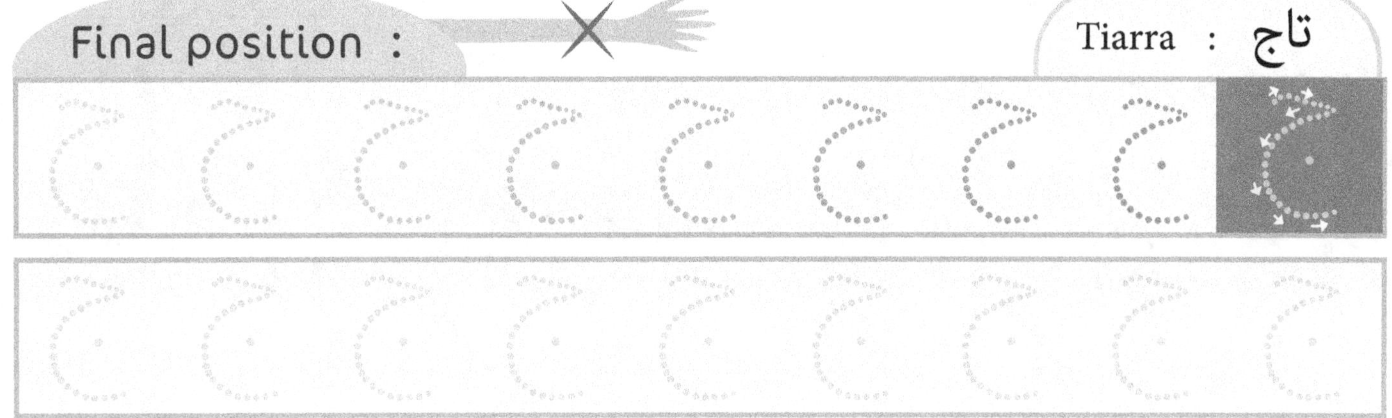

⊛ Let's practice !

Color the cirlces with letter Jeem :

Write the missing Jeem letter :

◎ اكتب حرف الجيم الناقص:

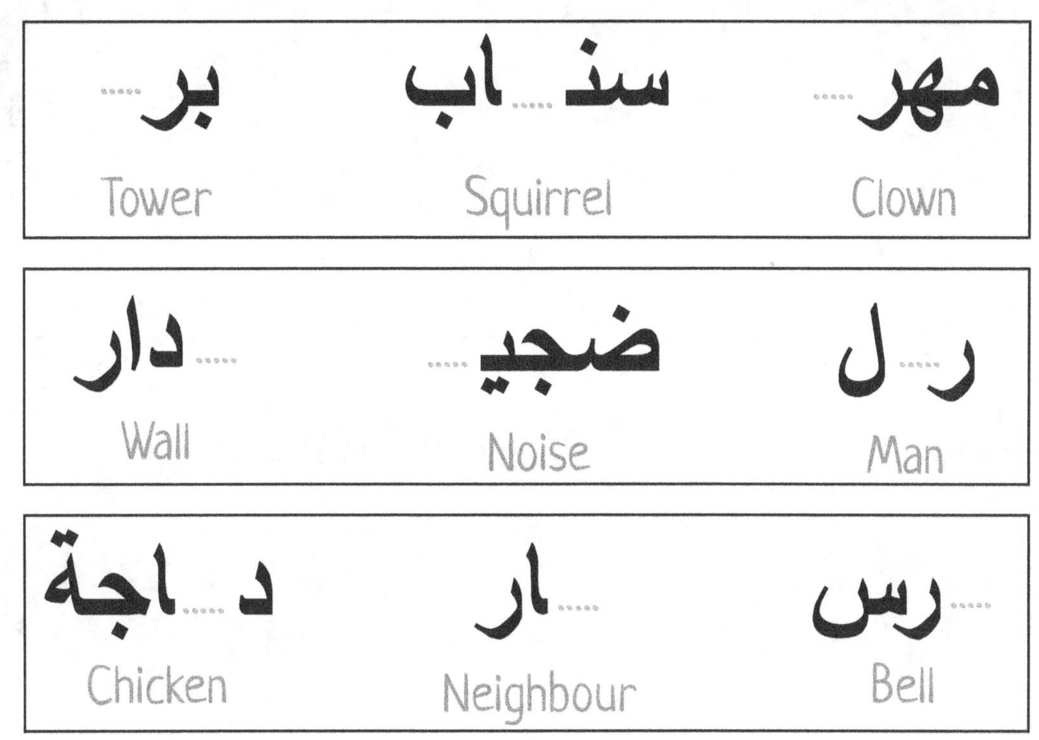

Trace, Color & learn!
MiLK
(Harf al haa)
حليب
Milk
حرف
6 الحاء : ح
Independent shape :
Whale : حوت
Initial position :
Meat : لحم
Medial position :

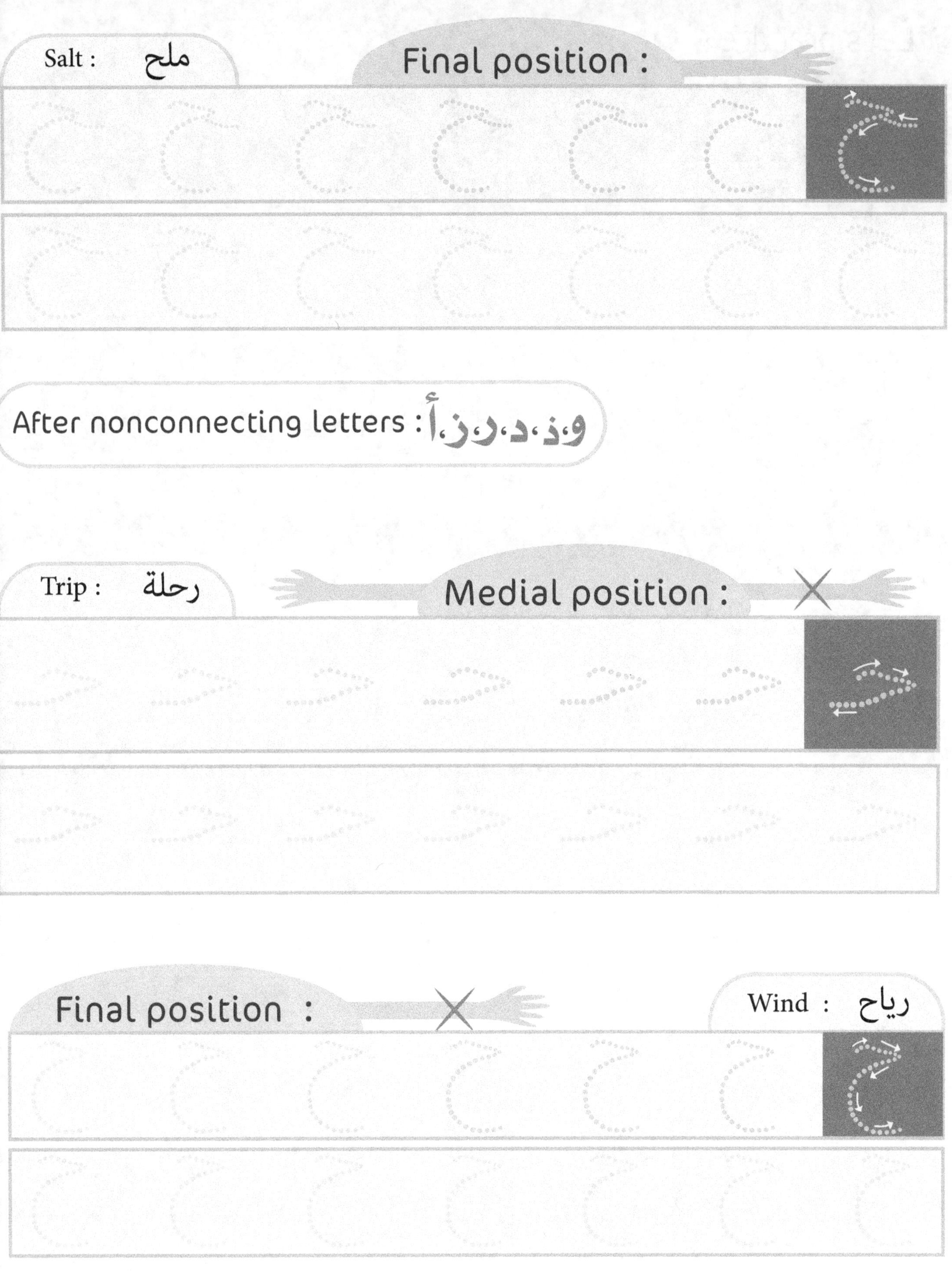

Salt : ملح
Final position :
After nonconnecting letters : و،ذ،د،ر،ز،أ
Trip : رحلة
Medial position :
Final position :
Wind : رياح

⊛ Let's practice !

⚙ Color the cirlces with letter Haa :

⚙ Write the missing Haa letter :   ⚙ اكتب حرف الحاء الناقص:

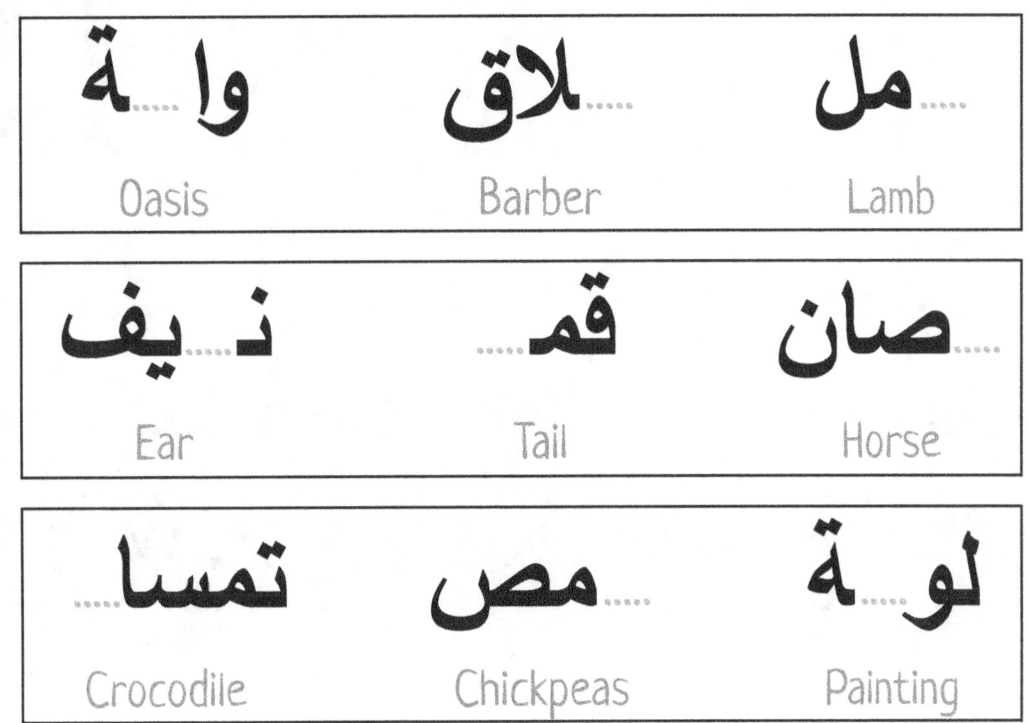

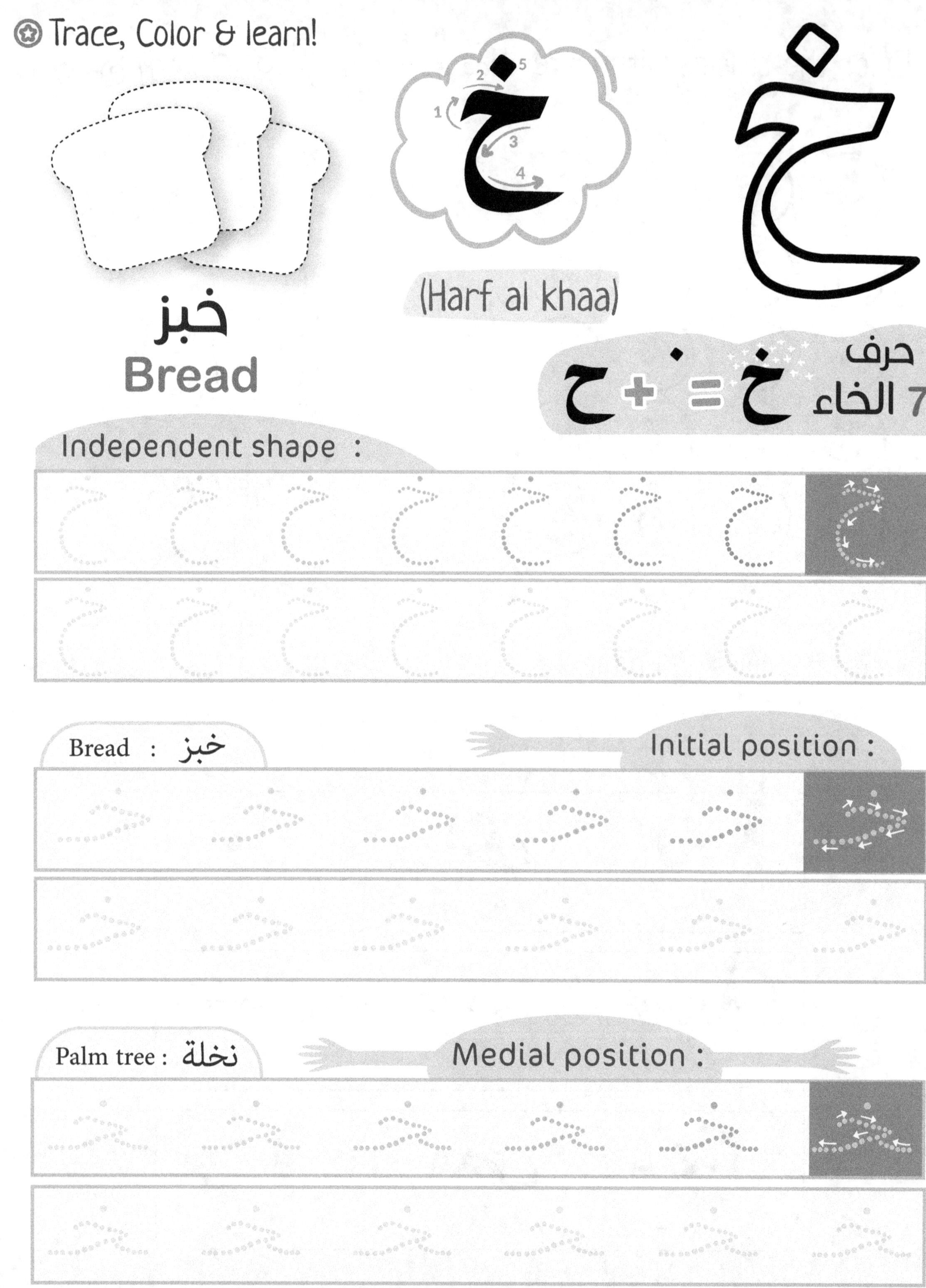

Independent shape :

Initial position :

Bread : خبز

Medial position :

Palm tree : نخلة

Watermelon : بطيخ
Final position :
After nonconnecting letters : و، ذ، د، ر، ز، أ
Hot : ساخن
Medial position :
Final position :
Weather : مناخ

اكتب حرف الخاء الناقص:

دراجة
Bike

(Harf al daal)

حرف
8 الدال **د**

Independent shape :

Bear : دب

Initial position :

School : مدرسة

Medial position :

Lion : أسد

After nonconnecting letters : أ،ز،ر،د،ذ،و

Tool : أداة

Fisher man : صياد

Let's practice !

Color the cirlces with letter Dal :

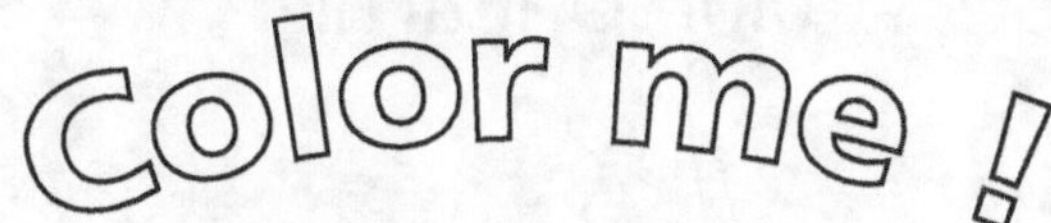

Bucket
دلو

Write the missing Dal letter :

اكتب حرف الدال الناقص:

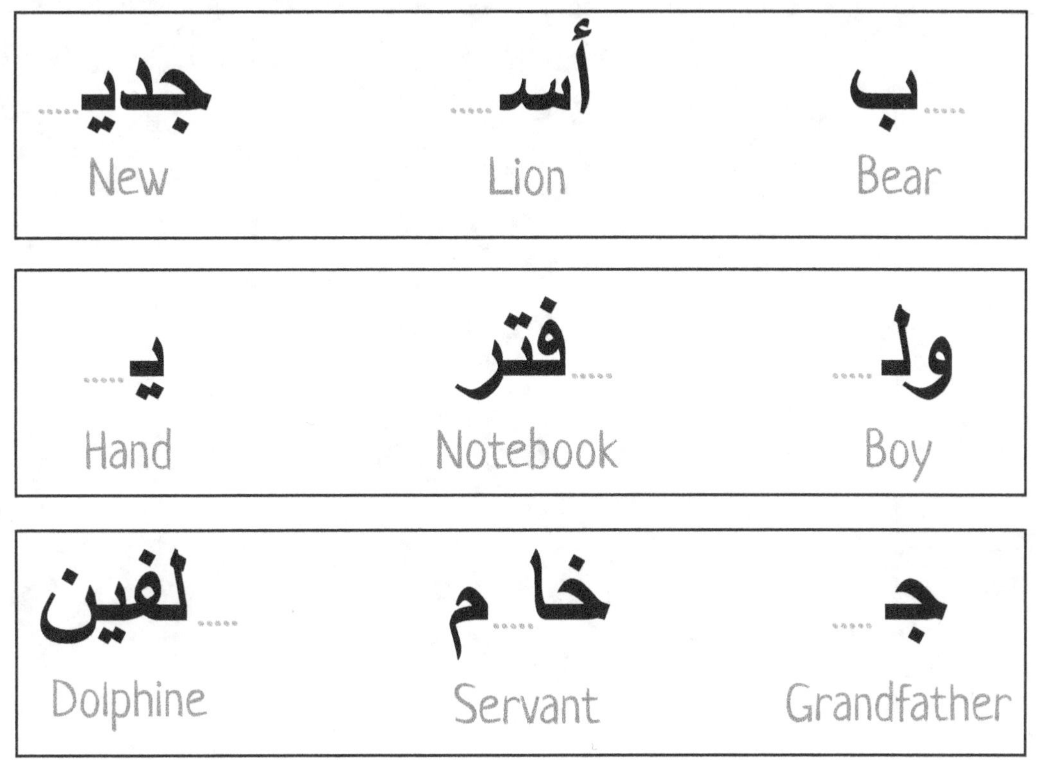

Trace, Color & learn!

(Harf al thaa)
ذيل
tail
حرف
9 الذال ذ
Independent shape :
Gold : ذهب
Initial position :
Root : جذر
Medial position :

Final position :

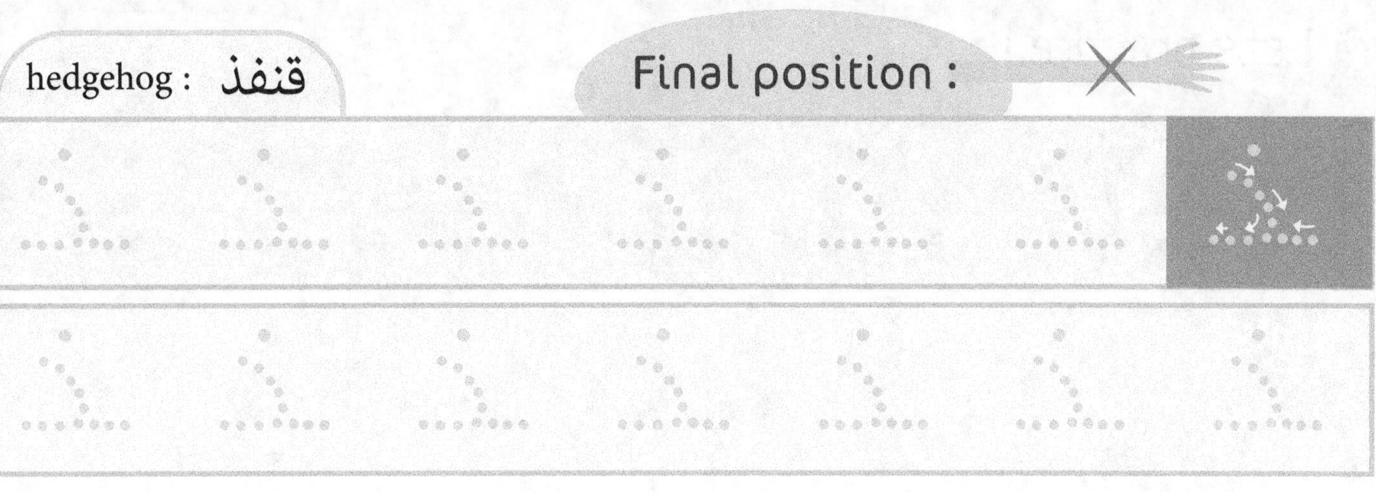

After nonconnecting letters : و، ذ، د، ر، ز، أ

Medial position :

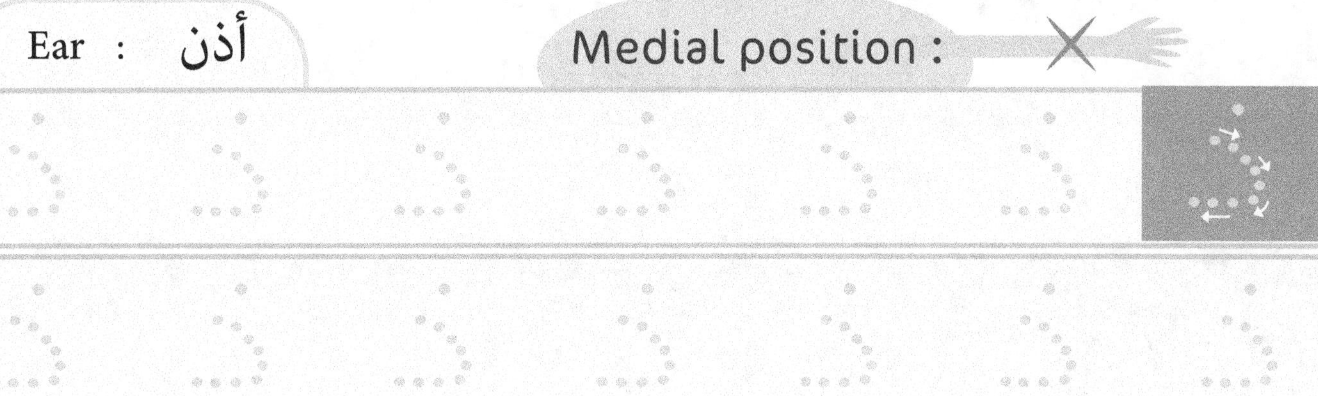

Final position :

hedgehog : قنفذ

⭐ # Let's practice !

Color the cirlces with letter Dhaal :

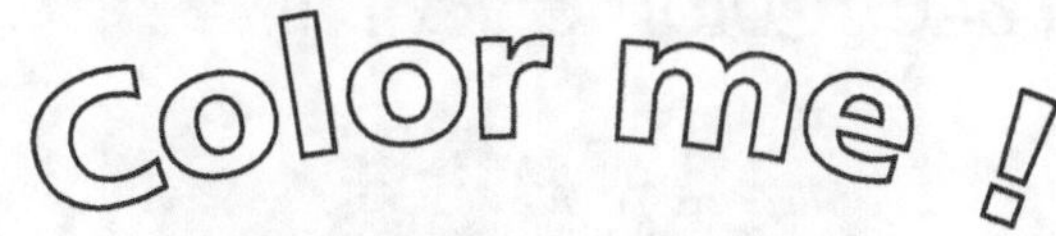

Write the missing Dhaal letter :

اكتب حرف الذال الناقص: ⚙

Trace, Color & learn!

ريشة
Feather

(Harf al raa)

حرف الراء 10

Independent shape :

Sand : رمل

Initial position :

Arabic : عربي

Medial position :

Sea : بحر

Final position :

Rose : وردة

Medial position :

Final position :

Breakfast : فطور

✪ Let's practice !

☀ Color the cirlces with letter Raa :

☀ Write the missing Raa letter :   اكتب حرف الراء الناقص:

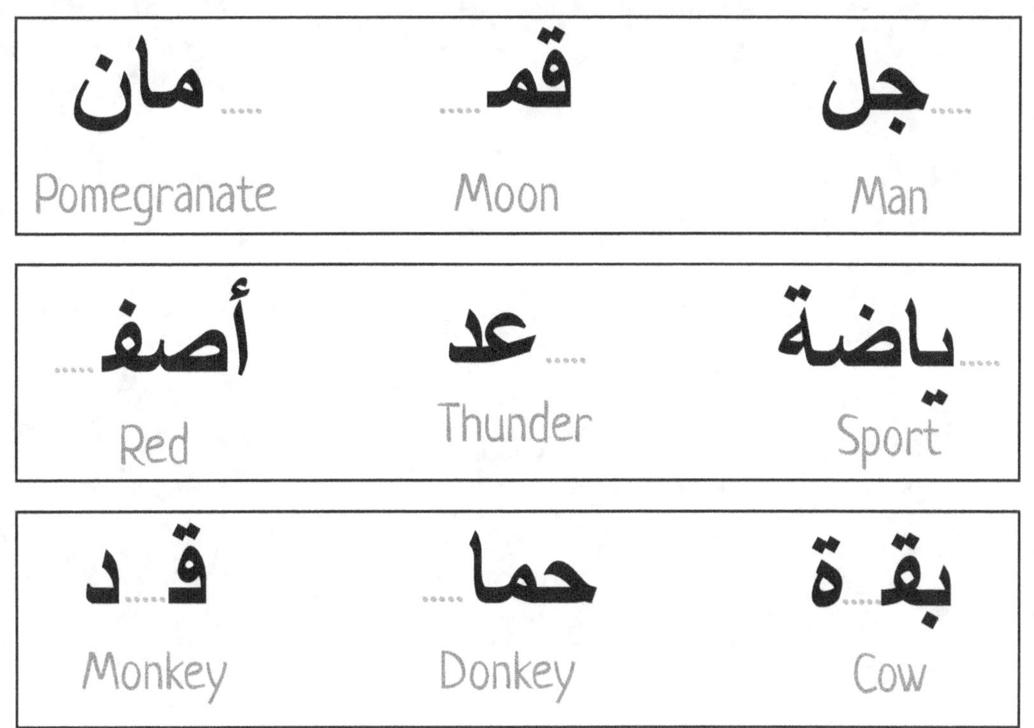

⭐ Trace, Color & learn!

ن
(Harf al zai)

ز

زربية
Carpet

حرف الزاي 11
ز = ن + ر

Independent shape :

Giraffe : زرافة
Initial position :

Butcher : جزار
Medial position :

Bread : خبز
Final position :

After nonconnecting letters : و،ذ،د،ر،ز،أ

Banana : موزة
Medial position :

Final position :
Cherries : كرز

⊛ Let's practice !

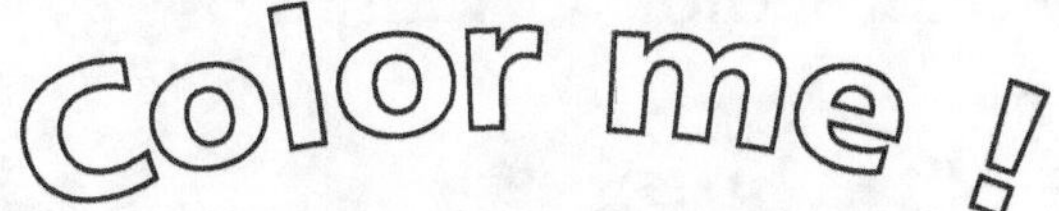

اكتب حرف الزاي الناقص:

(Harf seen)

ساعة
Clock

حرف السين س
12

Independent shape :

---

squirrel : سنجاب

Initial position :

Honey : عسل

Medial position :

Final position :

Medial position : ✕

Final position : ✕

⊛ Let's practice !

Color the cirlces with letter Seen :

Write the missing Seen letter :   اكتب حرف السين الناقص:

شمس
SUN

(Harf al sheen)

Independent shape :

Sun : شمس

Initial position :

Grass : عشب

Medial position :

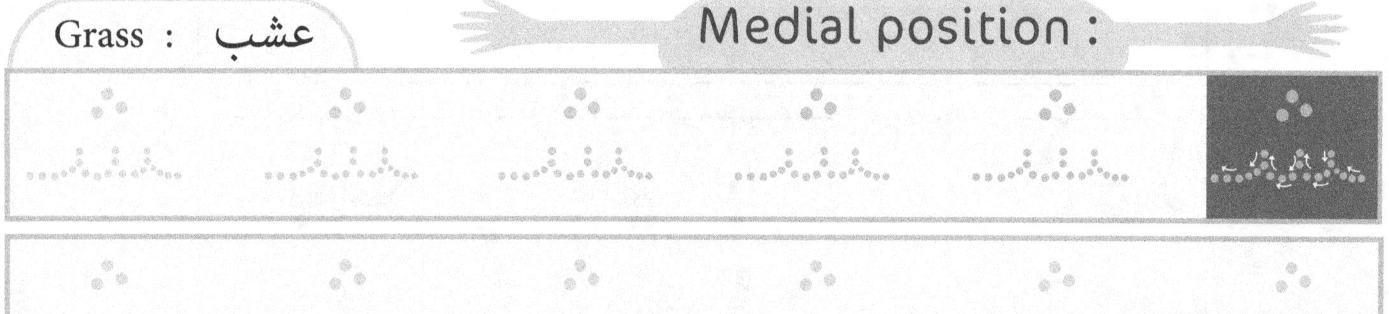

Nest : عش

Final position :

ـش ـش ـش ـش ـش

ـش ـش ـش ـش ـش ـش

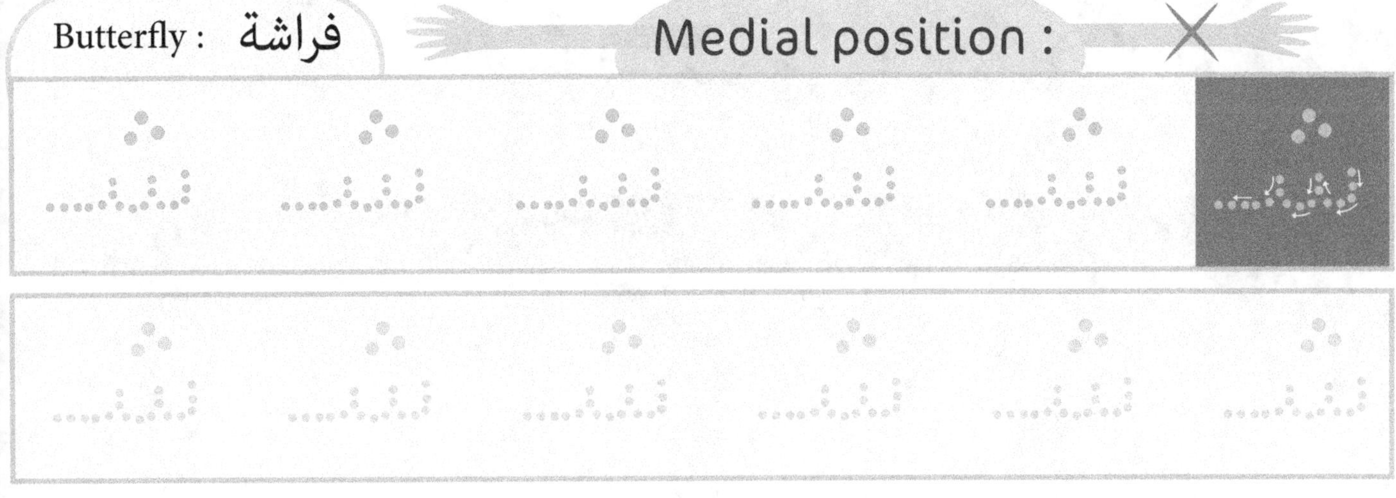

After nonconnecting letters : و،ذ،د،ر،ز،أ

Butterfly : فراشة

Medial position :

شـ شـ شـ شـ شـ

شـ شـ شـ شـ شـ شـ

Final position :

Bat : خفاش

ش ش ش ش ش

ش ش ش ش ش ش

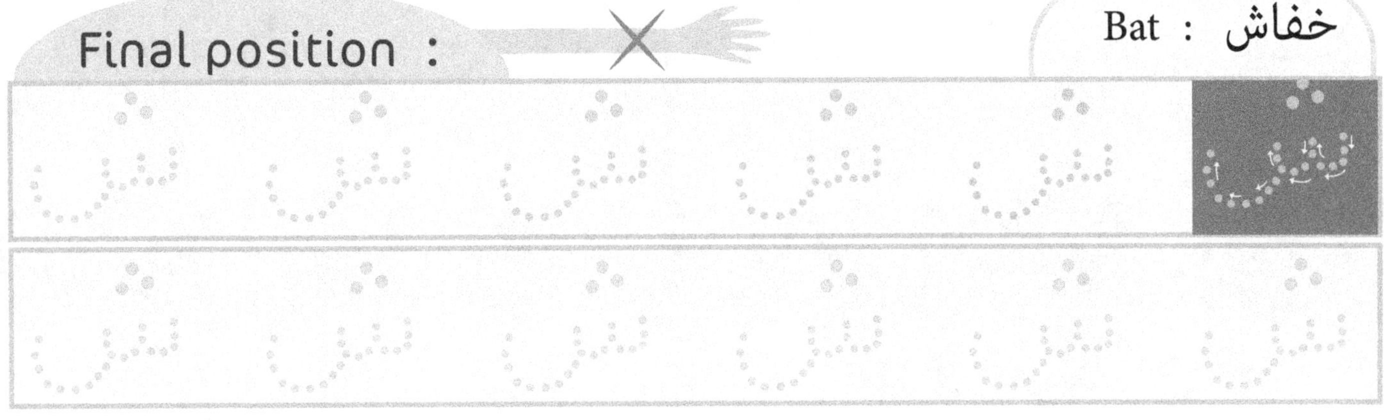

⊛ Let's practice !

Write the missing Sheen letter : ：اكتب حرف الشين الناقص

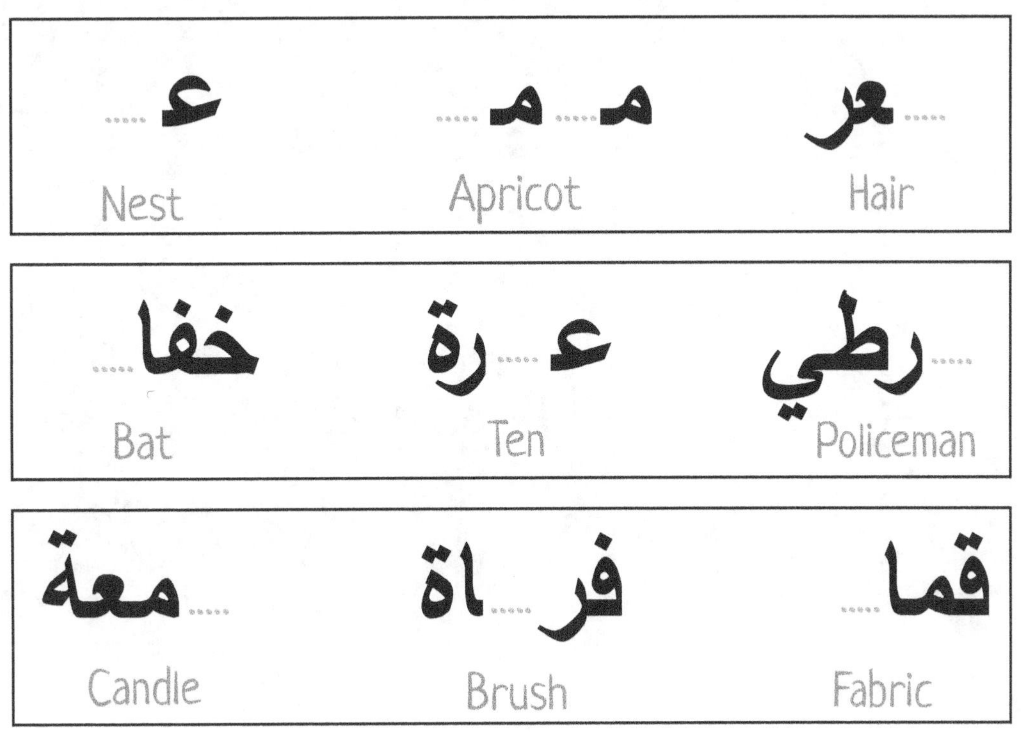

(Harf al saad)
حرف
الصاد ص 14
صبار
Cactus
Independent shape :
Morning : صباح
Initial position :
Onion : بصلة
Medial position :

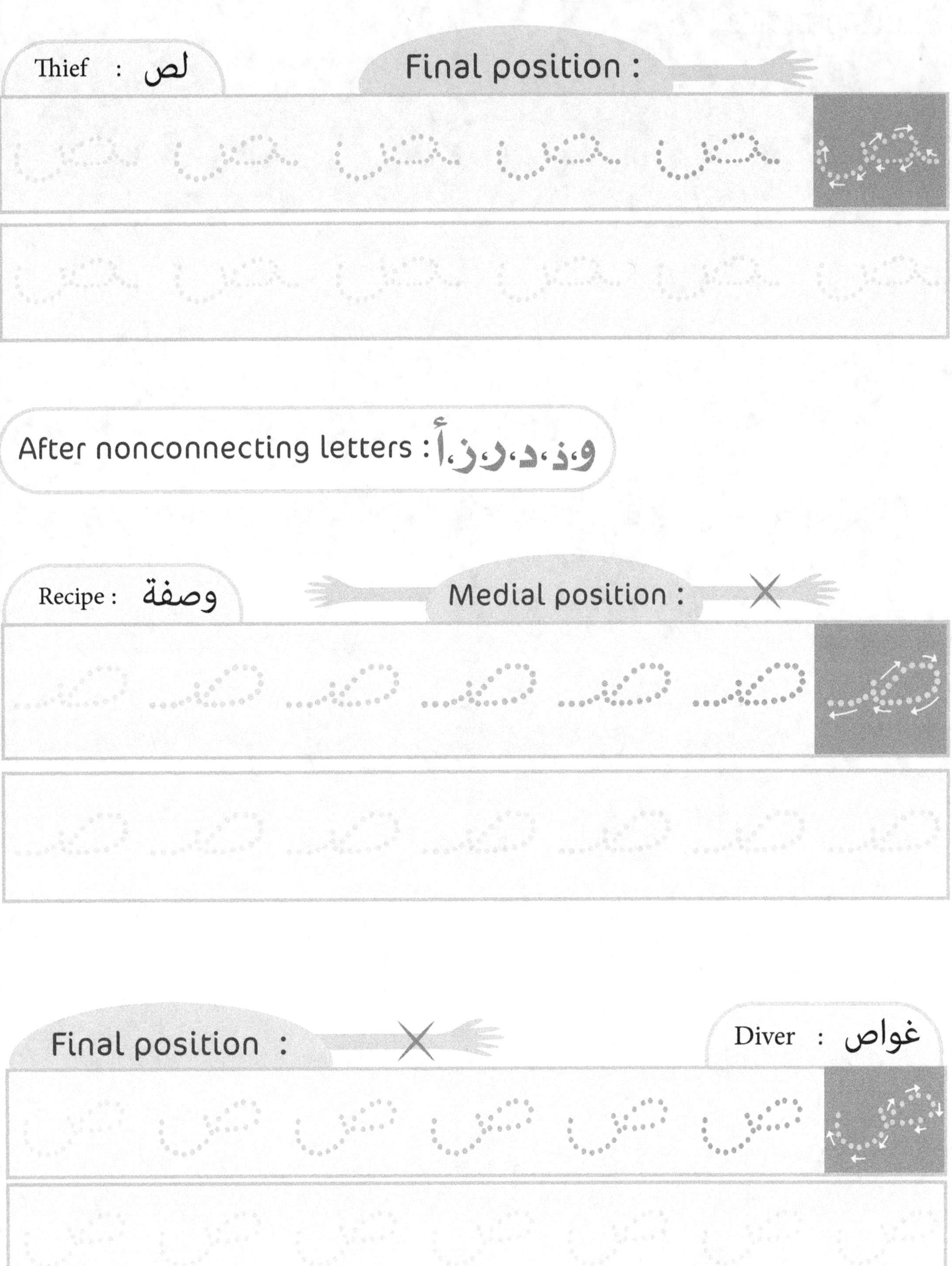

Thief : لص
Final position :
After nonconnecting letters : و،ذ،د،ر،ز،أ
Recipe : وصفة
Medial position :
Final position :
Diver : غواص

اكتب حرف الصاد الناقص:

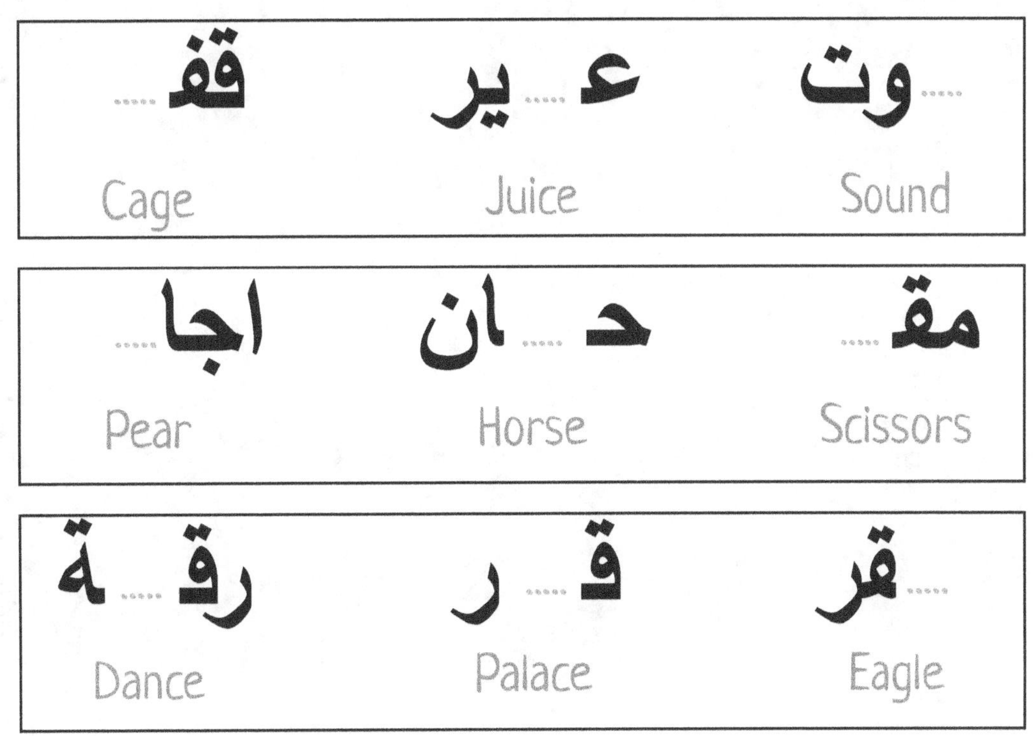

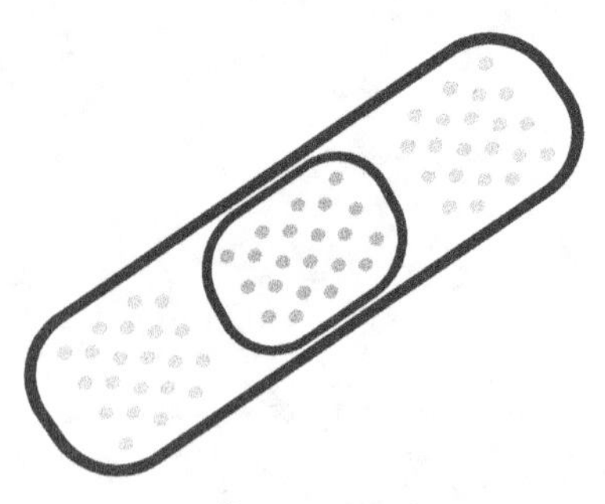

ضماد
Bandage

حرف الضاد ض = ٠ + ص 15

Independent shape :

Light : ضوء

Initial position :

Green : أخضر

Medial position :

Final position :

After nonconnecting letters : و،ذ،د،ر،ز،أ

Medial position :

Final position :

⊛ Let's practice !

⚙ Color the ciricles with letter Daad :

color me !

ض ب ض ح
ز ض هـ ض
ض د أ و
ش ث ض ص
ض س ف ض

Light
ضوء

⚙ Write the missing Daad letter :   ⚙ اكتب حرف الضاد الناقص:

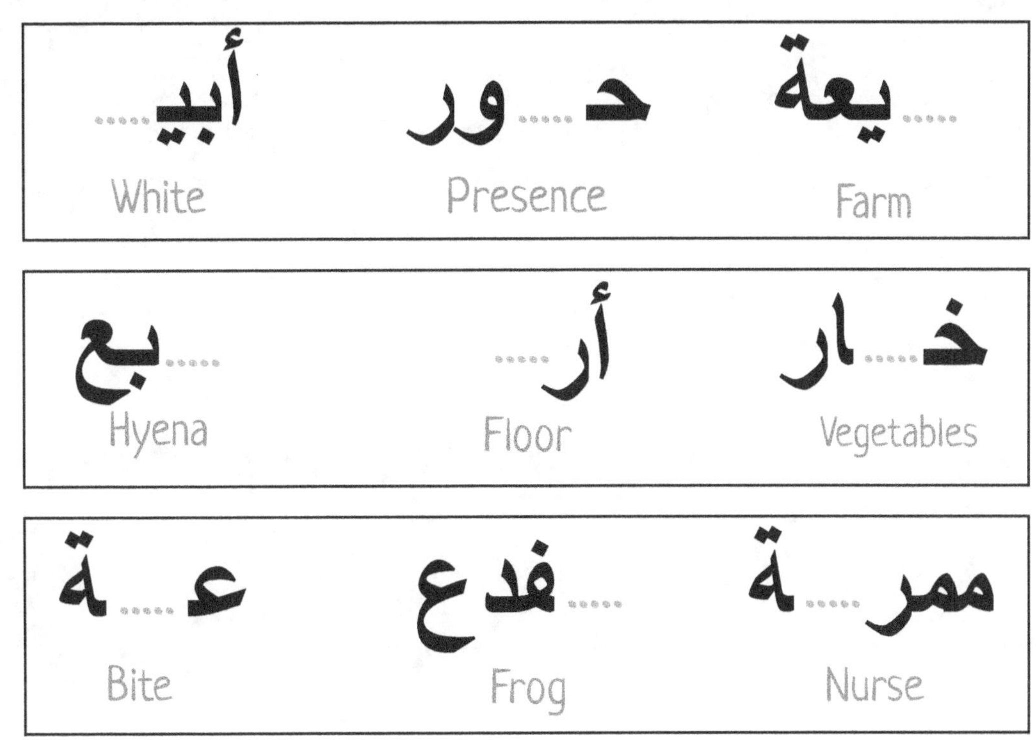

...يعة   حـ...ور   أبي...
Farm   Presence   White

خـ...ار   أر...   ...بع
Vegetables   Floor   Hyena

ممر...ة   ...فدع   عـ...ة
Nurse   Frog   Bite

⚅ Trace, Color & learn!

ط
1
2
6
3
5
4
(Harf al taa)

طبل
Drum

حرف
الطاء ط
16

Independent shape :

ط

Road : طريق

Initial position :

Duck : بطة

Medial position :

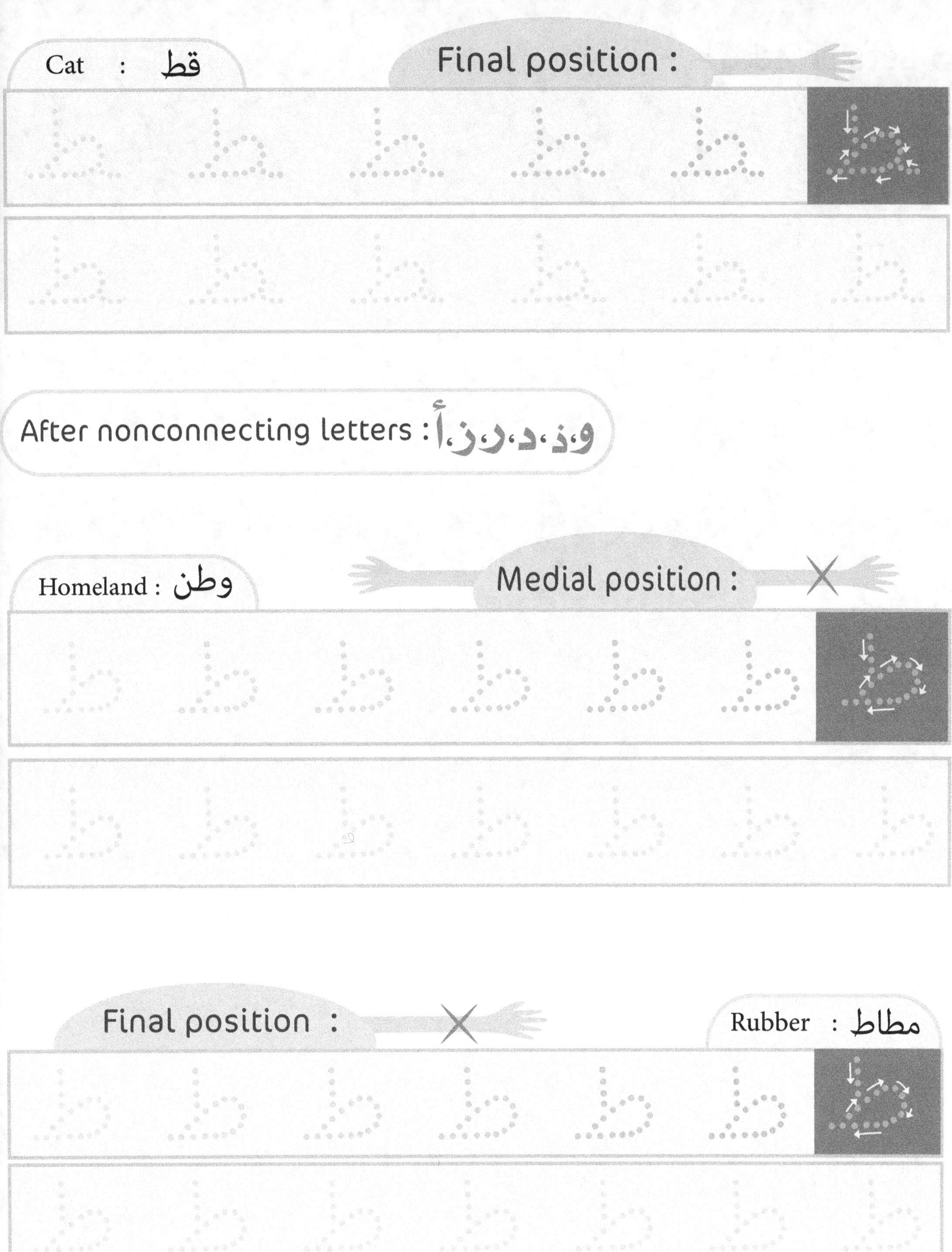
Cat : قط
Final position :
After nonconnecting letters : أ،ز،ر،د،ذ،و
Homeland : وطن
Medial position :
Final position :
Rubber : مطاط

✪ Let's practice !

Color the cirlces with letter Taa :

Write the missing Taa letter :

اكتب حرف الطاء الناقص:

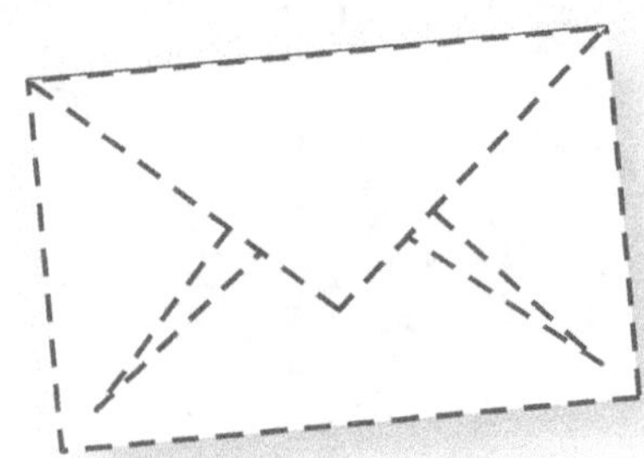

ظرف
Envelope

(Harf al dhaa)

Independent shape :

Initial position :

Moose : ظبي

Medial position :

Clean : نظيف

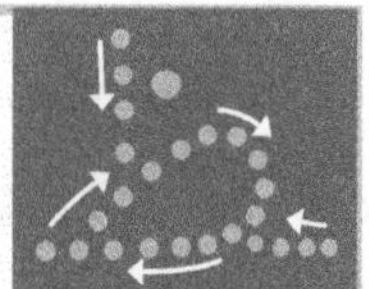

Final position :

Medial position :

Final position :

Write the missing Thaa letter :

اكتب حرف الظاء الناقص:

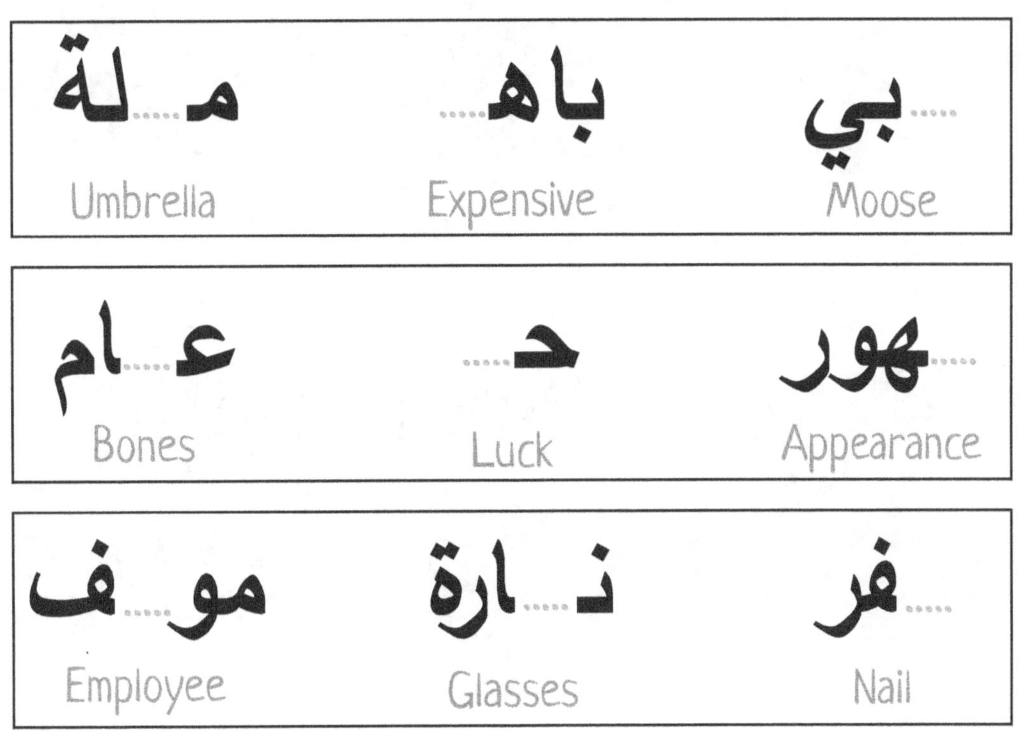

(Harf al Ein)

عنب
Grapes

حرف
العين ع
18

Independent shape :

Eye : عين

Initial position :

Cakes : كعك

Medial position :

Fun : ممتع

Final position :

After nonconnecting letters : و،ذ،د،ر،ز،أ

Forearm : ساعد

Medial position :

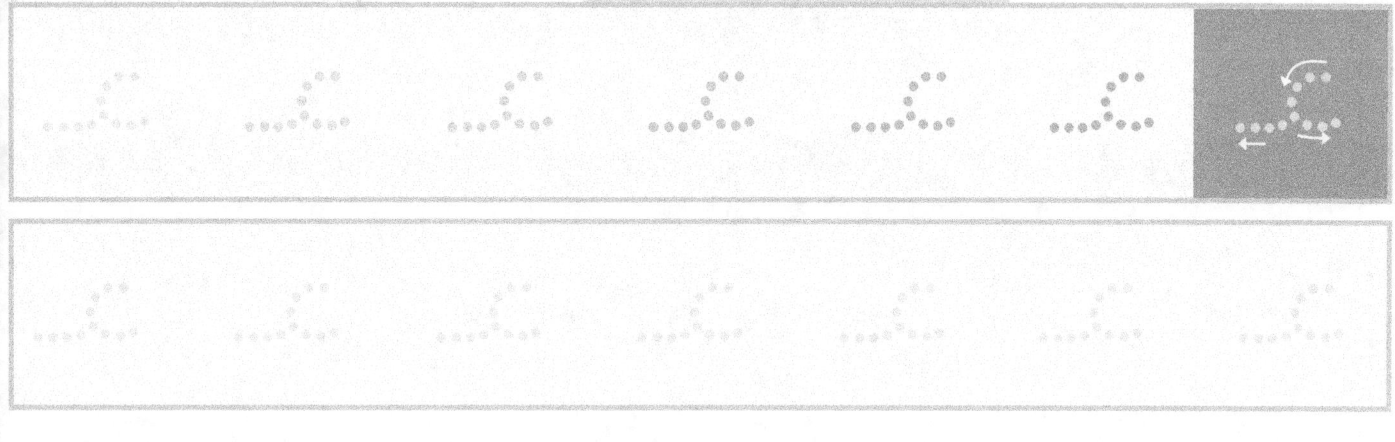

Final position :

Mint : نعناع

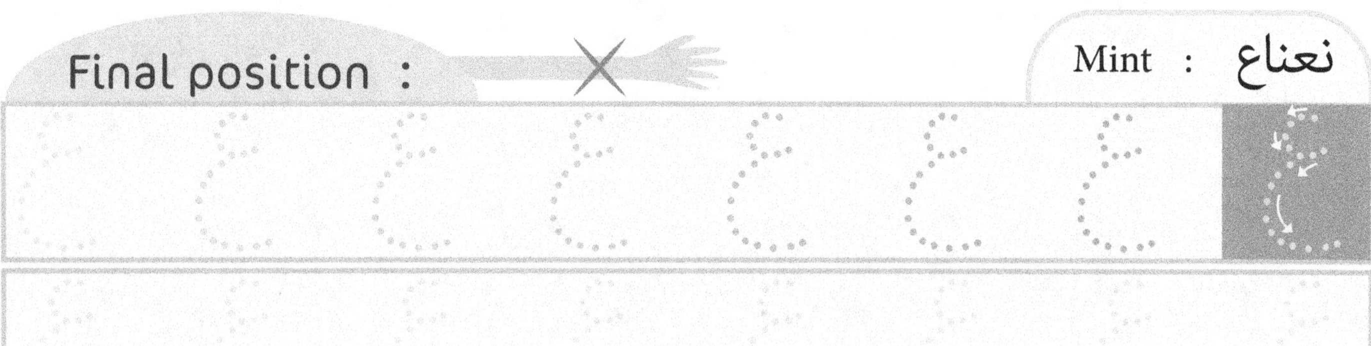

✪ Let's practice !

✿ Color the ciricles with letter Ein :

✿ Write the missing Ein letter :

اكتب حرف العين الناقص: ✿

صـ...ب	ضبـ...	...نب
Difficult	Hyena	Grapes
اصبـ...	شمـ...ة	قل...
Finger	Candle	Mind
دفا...	...سل	مل...قة
Defence	Honey	Spoon

حرف الغين 19   غ = ٠ + ع

Independent shape :

Initial position :

Cloud : غيمة

Medial position :

Small : صغير

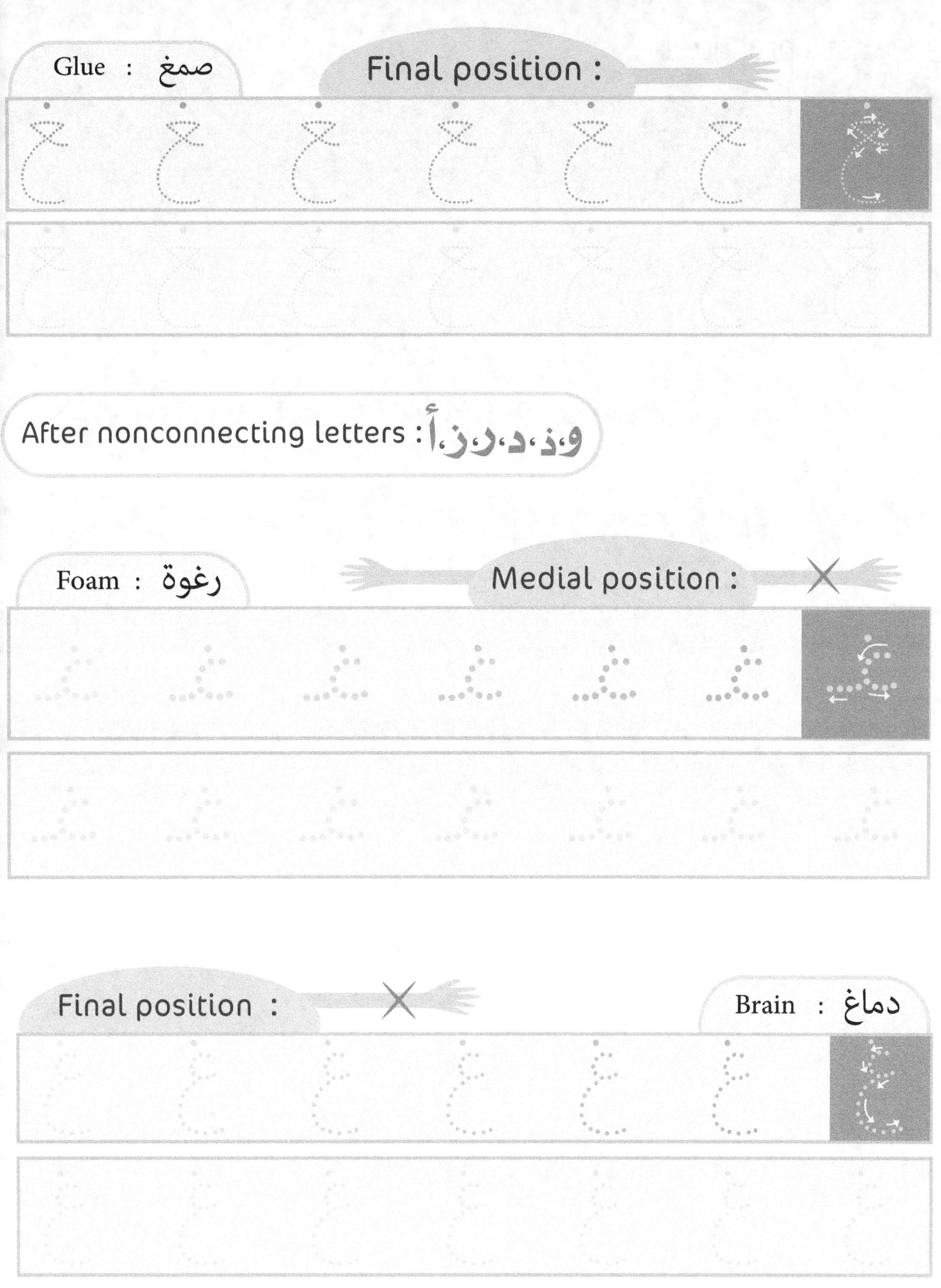

Glue : صمغ
Final position :
After nonconnecting letters : و،ذ،د،ر،ز،أ
Foam : رغوة
Medial position :
Final position :
Brain : دماغ

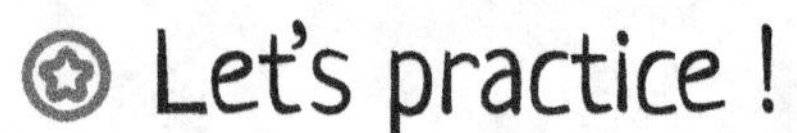 Let's practice !

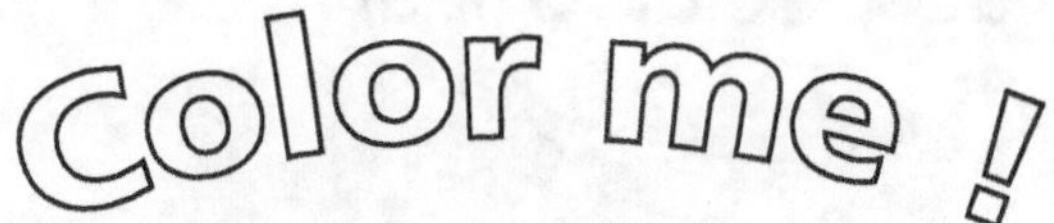

Write the missing Ghein letter :

اكتب حرف الغين الناقص:

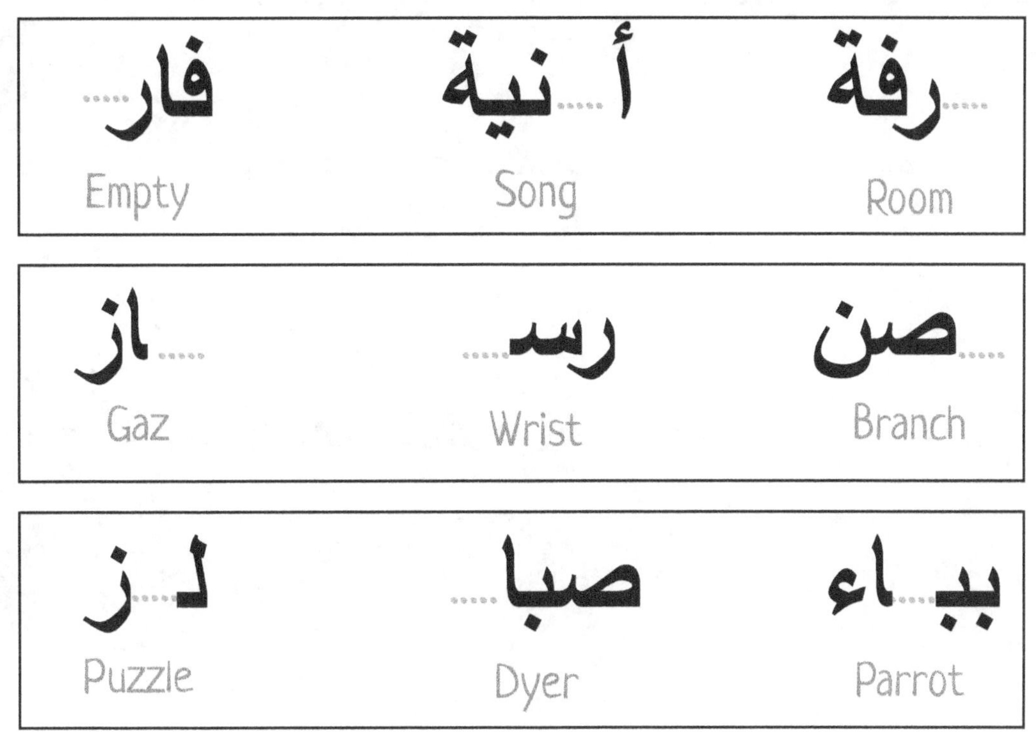

★ Trace, Color & learn!

ف ف
(Harf al faa)
1
2
3
4
5
6
ف
فلفل
PEPPER
حرف
الفاء ف
20
Independent shape :
Pepper : فلفل
Initial position :
Cage : قفص
Medial position :

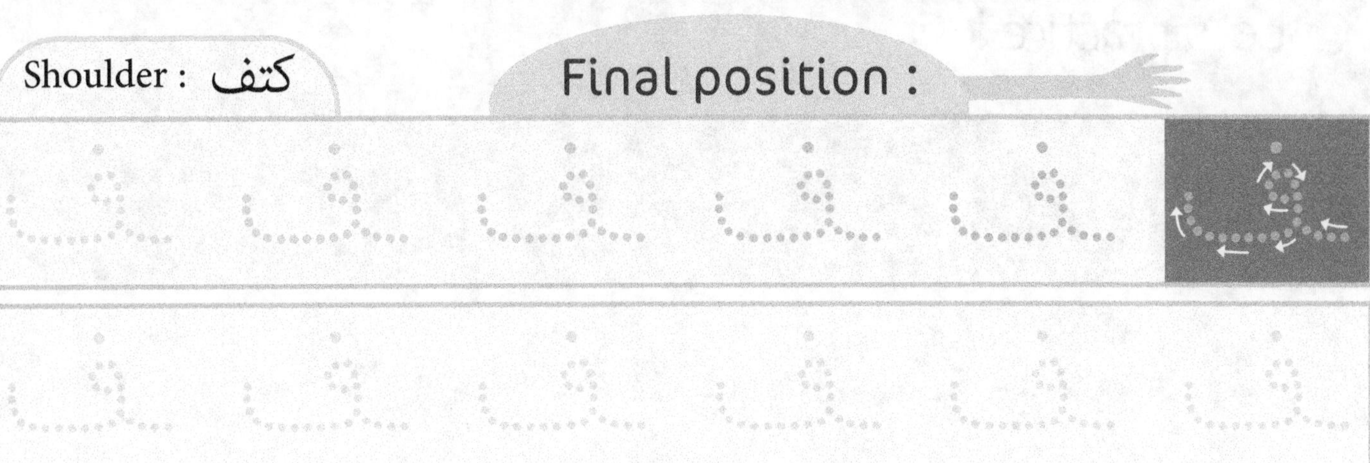

After nonconnecting letters : وذ، د، ر، ز، أ

☉ Let's practice !

Color the cirlces with letter Faa :

Write the missing Faa letter :

اكتب حرف الفاء الناقص:

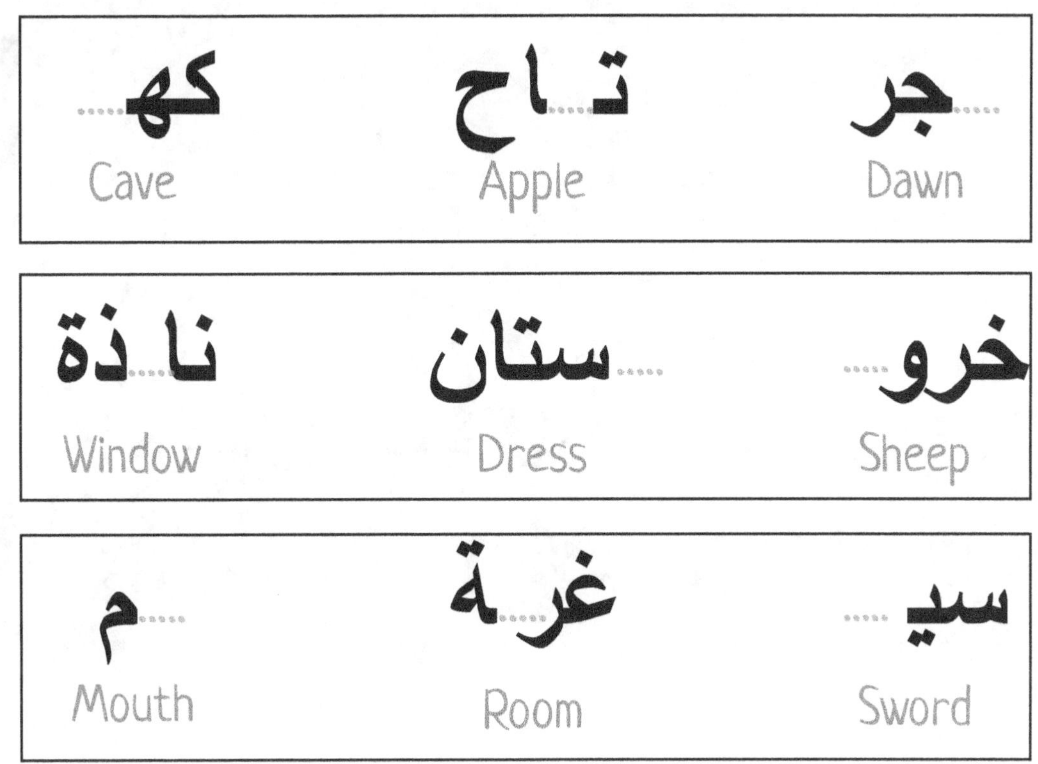

قمر
Moon

ق
(Harf al Qaf)

حرف القاف
21

Independent shape :

Short : قصير
Initial position :

Scissors : مقص
Medial position :

Tunnel : نفق

After nonconnecting letters : و، ذ، د، ر، ز، أ

Flour : دقيق

Leg : ساق

⊛ Let's practice !

☻ Color the cirlces with letter Qaf :

☻ Write the missing Qaf letter :

☻ اكتب حرف القاف الناقص:

كرة
Ball

(Harf al kaf)

حرف
الكاف 22
ك

Independent shape :

Dog : كلب

Initial position :

Sugar : سكر

Medial position :

Laughter : ضحك

Cunning : ماكر

Engine : محرك

⊛ Let's practice !

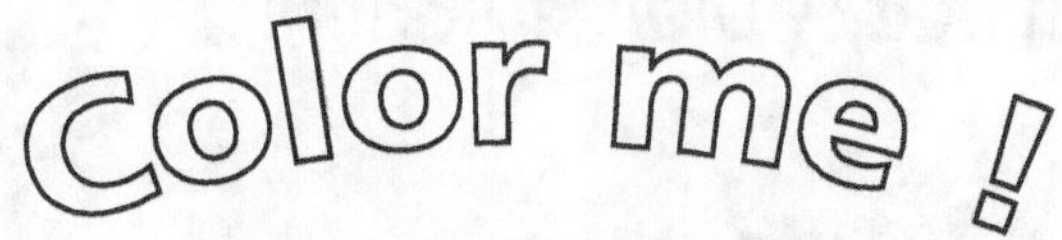

⊛ Color the cirlces with letter Kaf :

⊛ Write the missing Kaf letter : اكتب حرف الكاف الناقص: ⊛

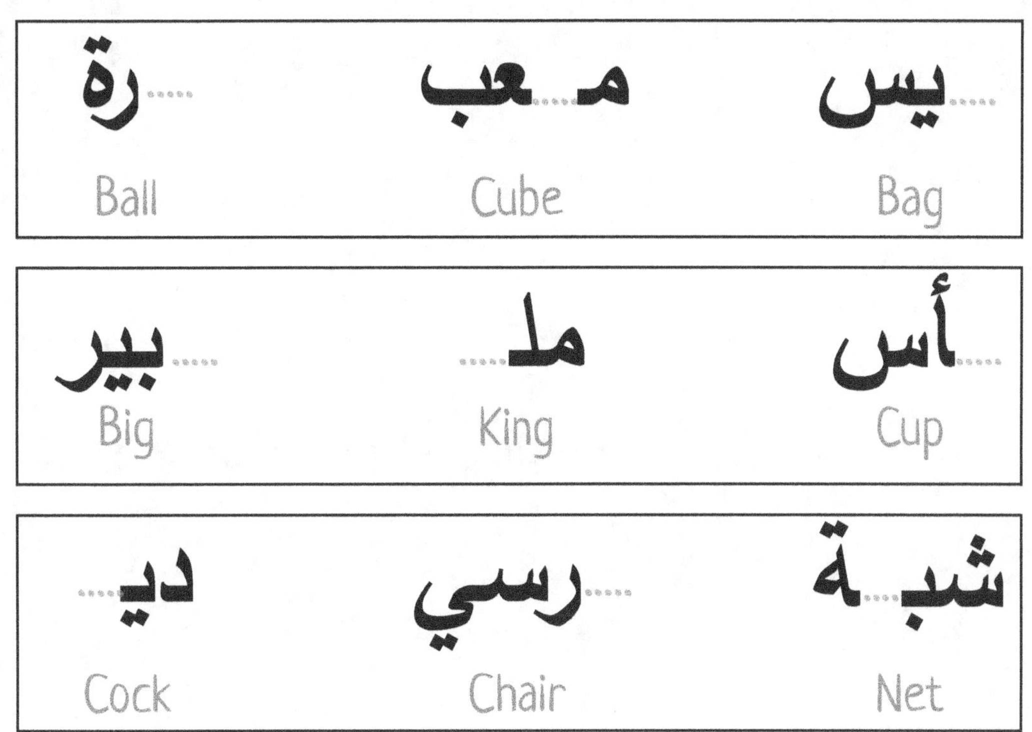

Trace, Color & learn!
ليمون
Lemon
(Harf al lam)
حرف اللام ل
23
Independent shape :
Lemon : ليمون
Initial position :
Heart : قلب
Medial position :

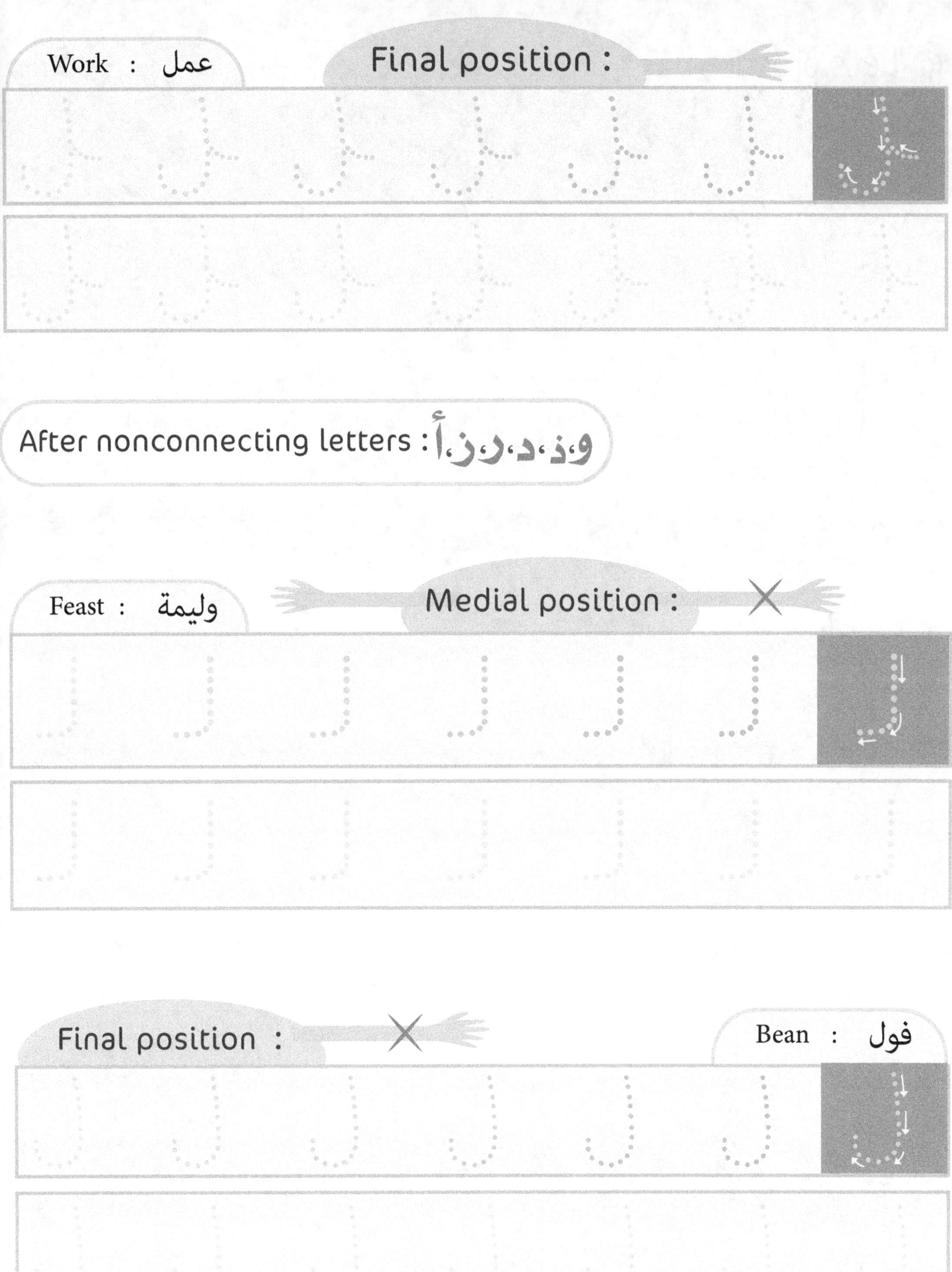

Work : عمل
Final position :
After nonconnecting letters : أ،ز،ر،د،ذ،و
Feast : وليمة
Medial position :
Final position :
Bean : فول

✪ Let's practice !

Write the missing Lam letter :

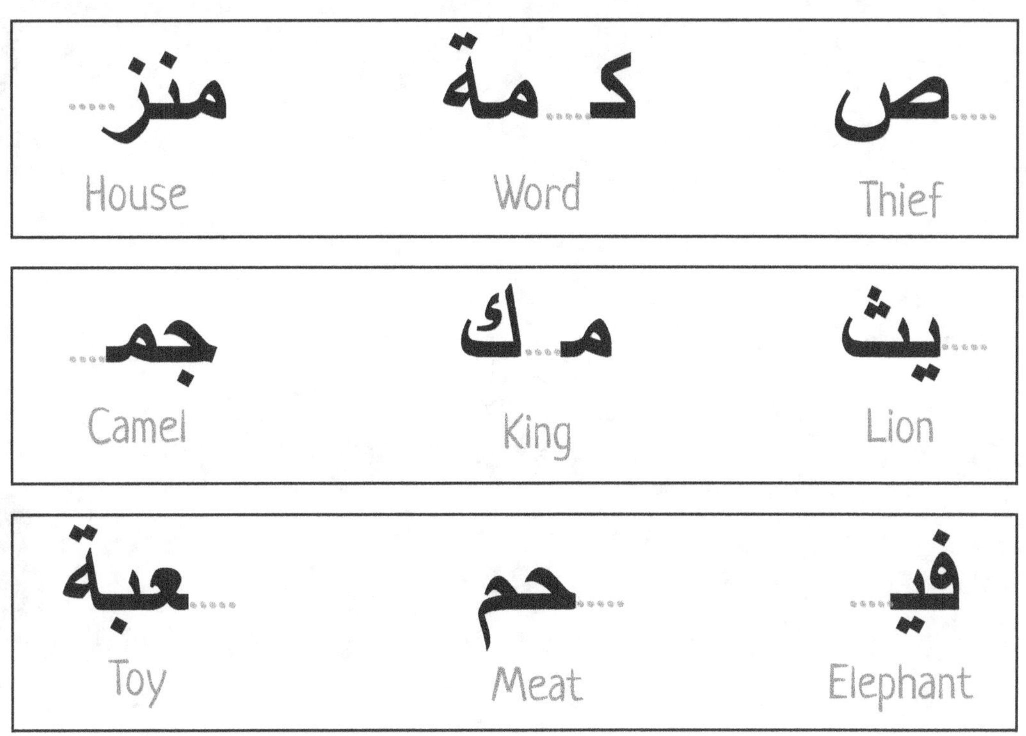

مظلة
Umbrella

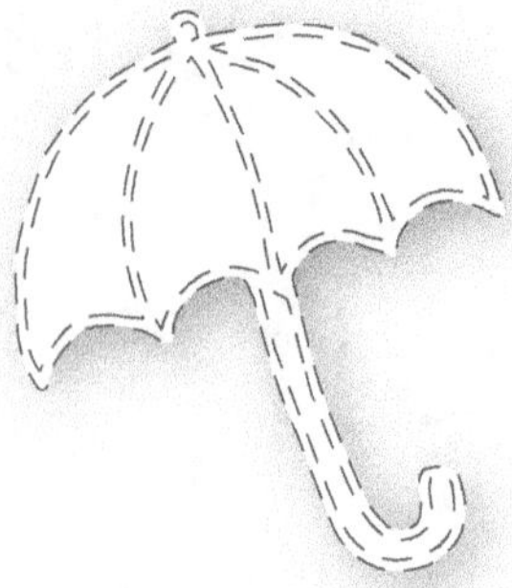

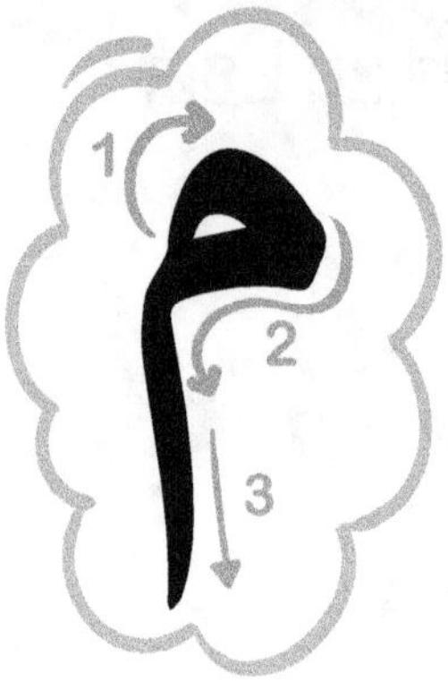

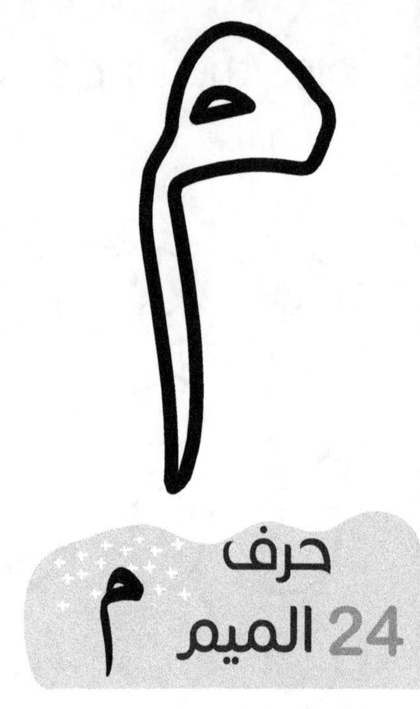

Independent shape :

Initial position :

Scissors : مقص

Medial position :

Beautiful : جميل

Pencil : قلم

Final position :

After nonconnecting letters : وذ،د،ر،ز،أ

Hope : أمل

Medial position : ✕

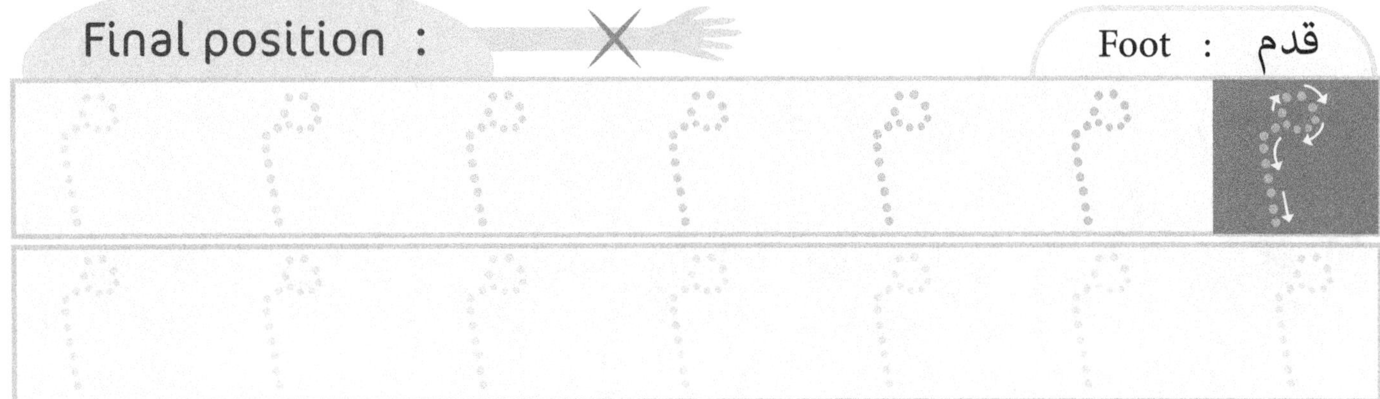

Final position : ✕

Foot : قدم

✪ Let's practice !

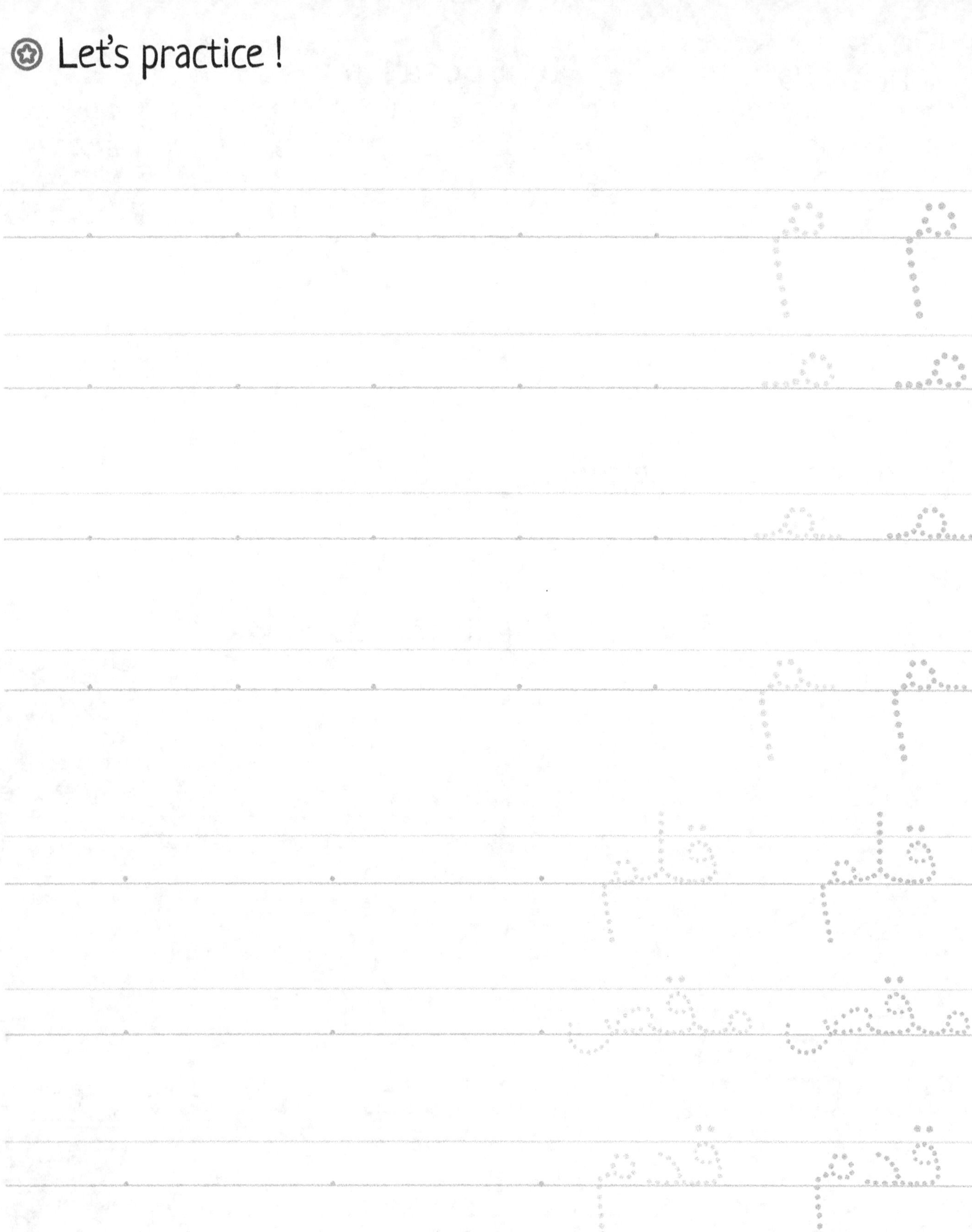

Color the cirlcles with letter Meem :

Write the missing Meem letter :

اكتب حرف الميم الناقص:

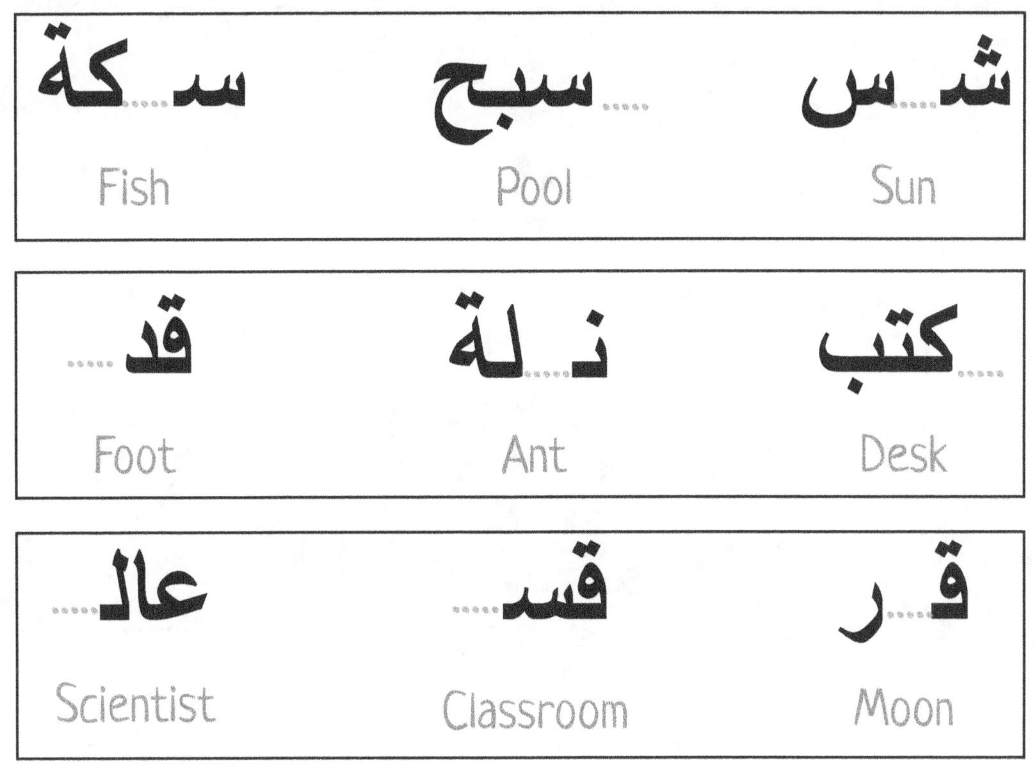

سد....كة	سبح....	شـ....س
Fish	Pool	Sun
....قد	نـ....لة	كتب....
Foot	Ant	Desk
عال....	قسـ....د	قـ....ر
Scientist	Classroom	Moon

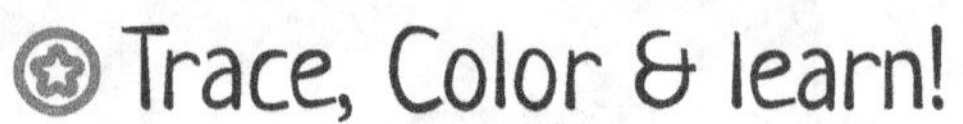

نخلة
Palm Tree

Independent shape :

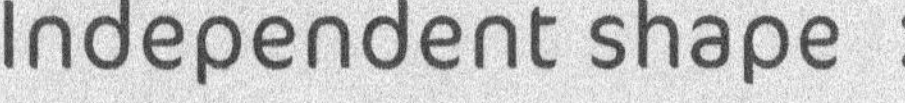

Eagle : نسر

Initial position :

Grapes : عنب

Medial position :

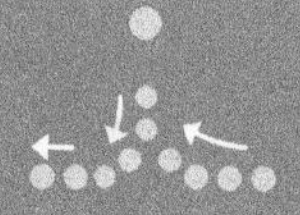

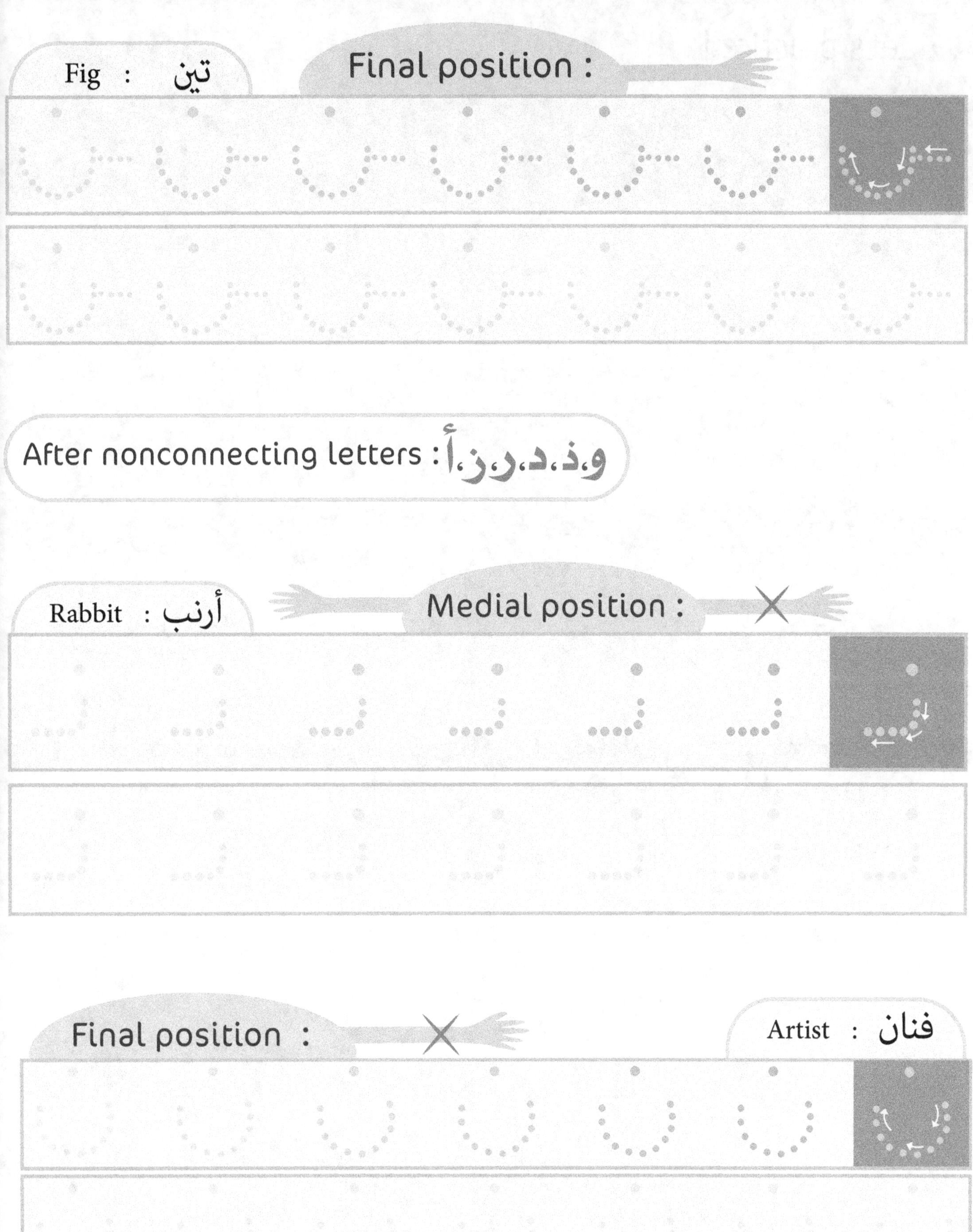

Fig : تين
Final position :
After nonconnecting letters : و،ذ،د،ر،ز،أ
Rabbit : أرنب
Medial position :
Final position :
Artist : فنان

⊕ Let's practice !

⚙ Write the missing Noon letter : ⚙ اكتب حرف النون الناقص:

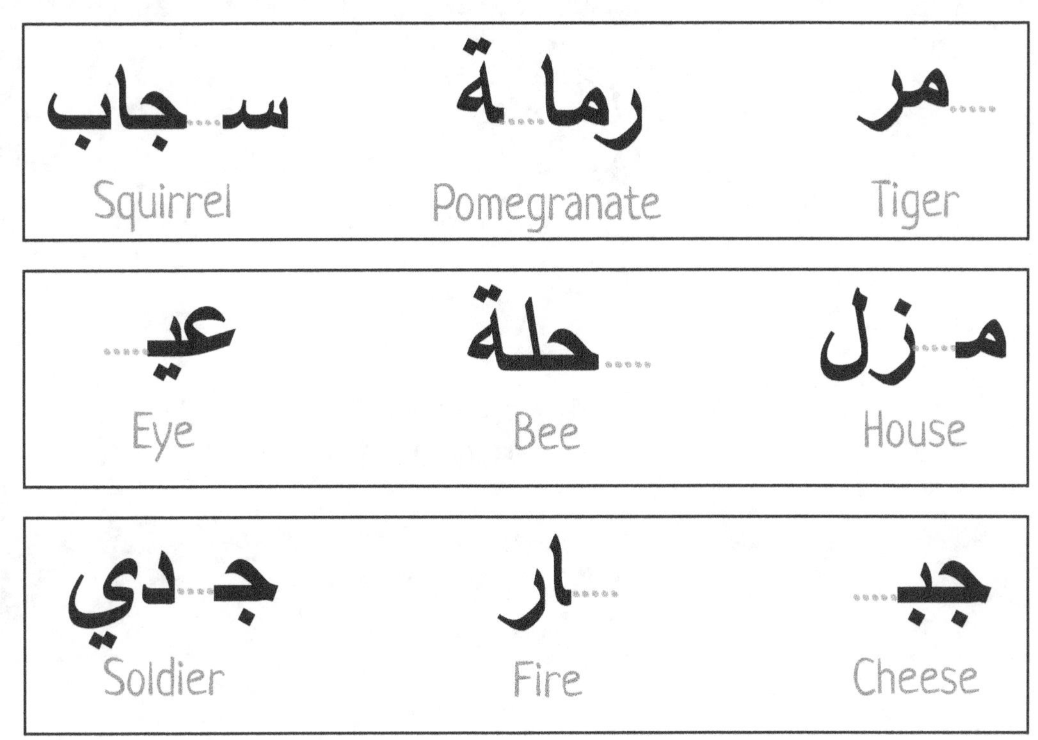

هدية
Gift

(Harf al Haa)

حرف
الهاء **هـ** 26

Independent shape :

Goal : هدف

Initial position :

River : نهر

Medial position :

Alarm clock : منبه

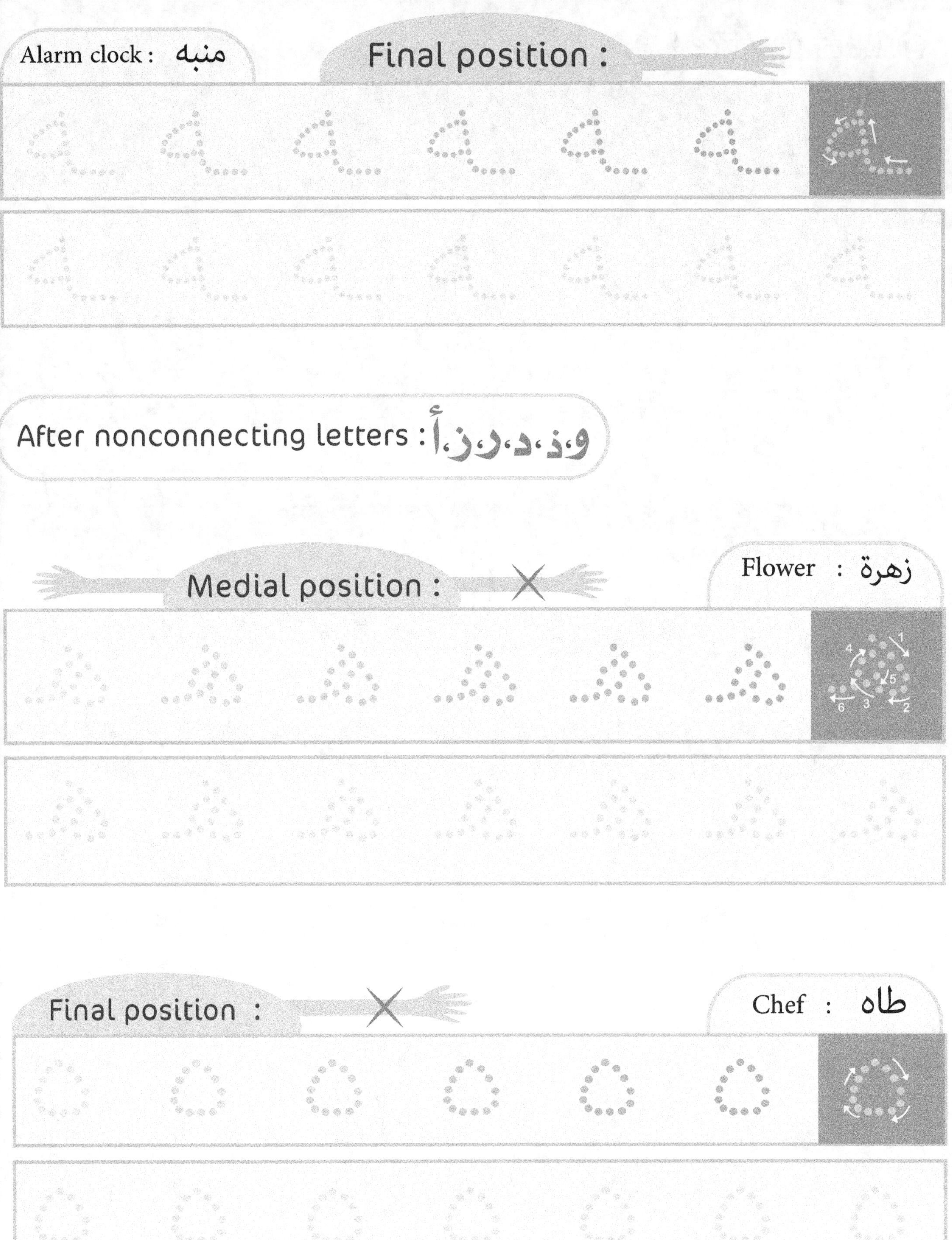

Let's practice !

Color the cirlces with letter Haa :

Write the missing Haa letter :

اكتب حرف الهاء الناقص:

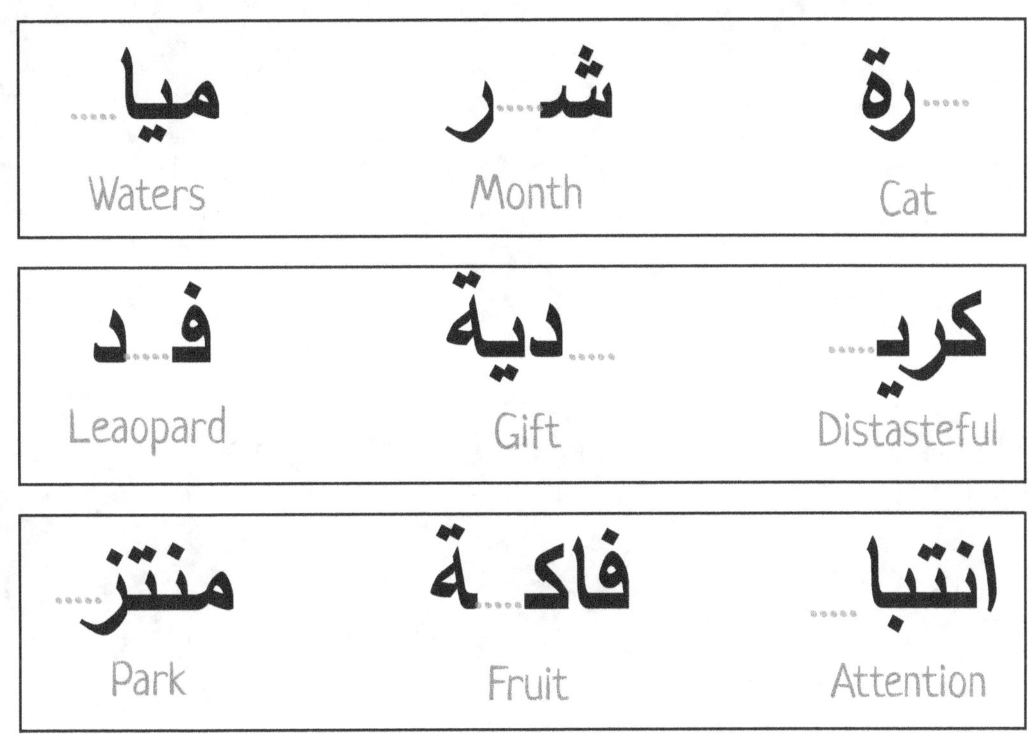

(Harf al waw)

وردة
Rose

حرف
الواو 27
و

Independent shape :

Rose : وردة

Initial position :

Banana : موزة

Medial position :

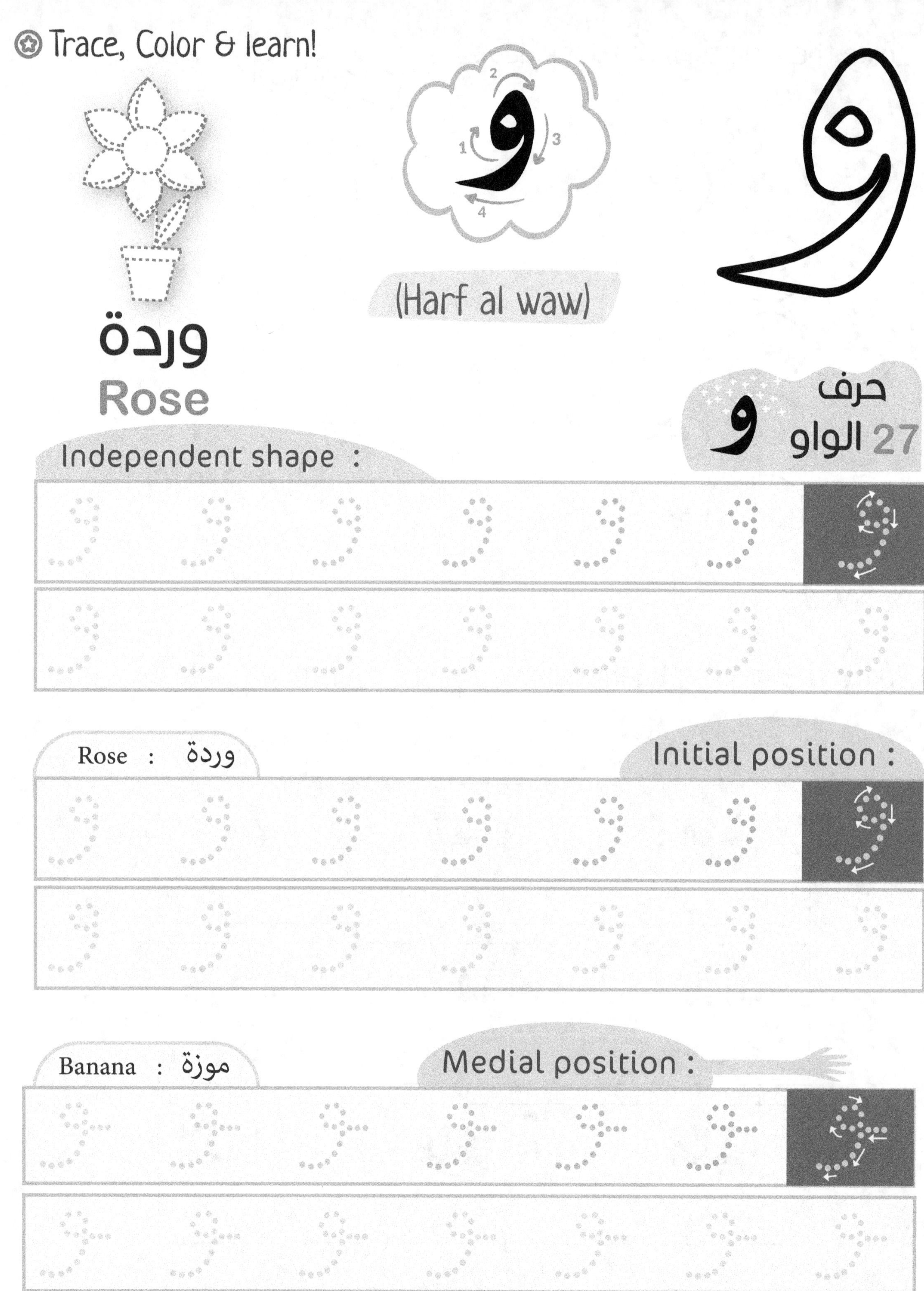

Final position :
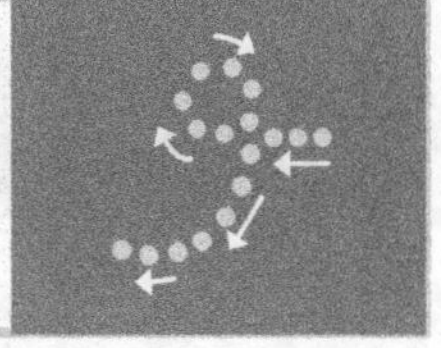

After nonconnecting letters : أ،ز،ر،د،ذ،و

Medial position :

Final position :

⊛ Let's practice !

Write the missing Waw letter :

اكتب حرف الواو الناقص:

Trace, Color & learn!
يد
Hand
(Harf al yaa)
حرف الياء 28
ي
Independent shape :
Hand : يد
Initial position :
Elephant : فيل
Medial position :

Boy : صبي

Final position :

After nonconnecting letters : و،ذ،د،ر،ز،أ

Oil : زيت

Medial position :

Final position :

Tea : شاي

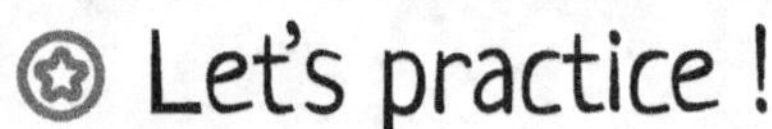 Let's practice !

Color the ciricles with letter Yaa :

Write the missing Yaa letter :   اكتب حرف الياء الناقص:

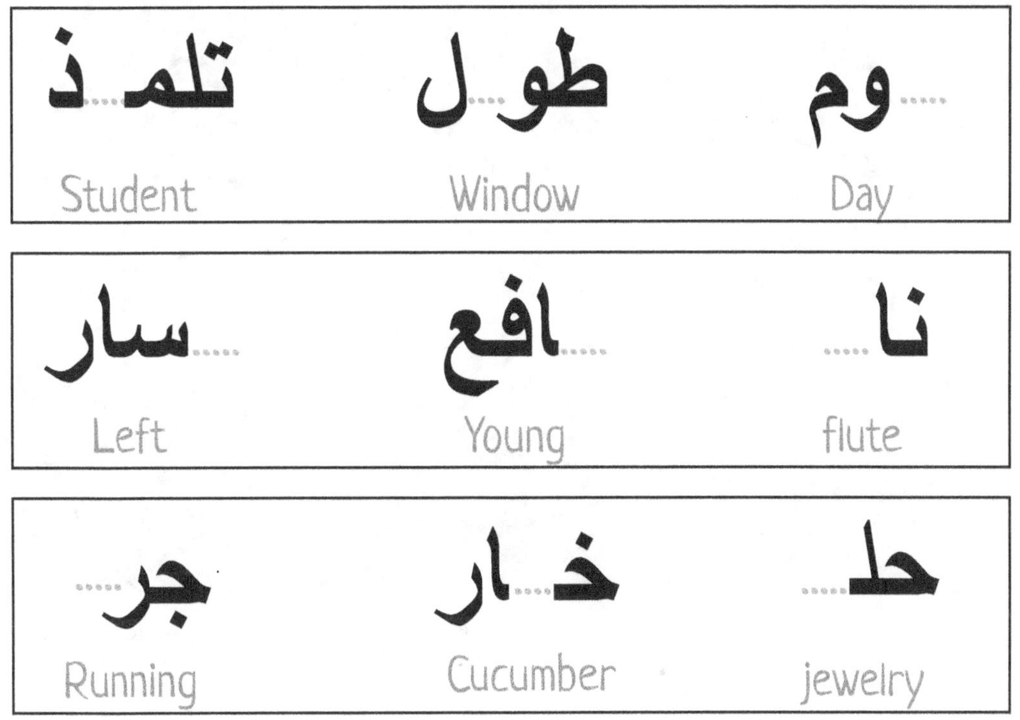

WELL DONE !

Name : ___________________

Is hereby congratulated for completing

ARABIC LETTERS TRACING

Workbook